Southern Keto Cookbook

100 Southern Keto Recipes for a Healthy Life (A Keto Comfort Foods Book)

Adriana Hildebrandt

ISBN-13: 979-8668993895

DEDICATION

To all who desire to live life to the fullest!

TABLE OF CONTENT

INTRODUCTION

An assortment of motivations from such a significant number of developments around the globe has made the southern food what it is in our day. Basically, southern food has its beginnings in the neighborhood and intriguing elements of the indigenous populace and those acquired from outsiders. Believe it or not, great management and prioritization are at the center of the southern eating routine.

The southern eating routine underlines staples, for example, peaches, sweet potatoes, peanuts, pecans, kale, turnips, mustard, collards, black-eyed peas and okra. Local games, for example, squirrel, rabbit, opossum, and seafood which incorporates Mississippi catfish, crab, crawfish, shrimp, and clams were a significant wellspring of sustenance and nourishment in the southern diet. Chicken and pork were likewise a primary element in the early long stretches of the southern eating routine.

Regardless, the southern eating routine has gotten extremely assorted throughout the years with little increments of flavors to a great extent. This diverseness of the southern eating regimen was brought into being by the evolving socioeconomics. The previously mentioned reasons and more have added to the advancement of the southern eating routine into what it is today, achieving absolutely novel cooking styles.

The southern-keto diet is a mix of the notable health diet, the ketogenic diet, and the flavorful deliciousness of the southern food in one bundle. You would now be able to have the advantages of the ketogenic diet while getting a charge out of conventional southern dinners at the same time. Actually, it is a 2-in-1 bundle that gives you a more extensive assortment of food alternatives to pick from, holding the inventiveness of the southern way of eating and furthermore giving you access to the advantage of arriving at nutritional ketosis.

Regardless of what catches your fancy on the southern keto diet, be it the ketogenic diet, the southern diet, or both... you will be set up for a healthy meal experience that won't just tempt your taste buds, but it will demonstrate the rich and differing social history of the south. What's more, it will guarantee wellbeing and quick and healthy weight loss. You will appreciate the upsides of the southern keto while you are grinding away!

The Basics of the Southern Diet and the Ketogenic Diet

One of the longest standing staples of the south is the sweet tea, made with black tea and served chilled. You should add in your most loved keto sweetener while the tea is hot and mix until sweetener-syrup is diffused all through the tea

In the southern diet, sauces are not the same throughout the South. You will probably come across a mustard-centered sauce that is common in South Carolina, while a vinegar-centered sauce is favored in North Carolina. Likewise, bar-b-ques differ across the south. In Texas, a mesquite-smoked brisket is favored, while North and South Carolinas will favor pulled pork shoulders or ribs.

Red-eye gravy otherwise called cedar gravy is a thin sauce that is often seen in Southern food. This is made with leftover coffee mixed with pan drippings. These pan drippings are gotten from frying intensely salted ham was cured and smoked. This gravy is also a major part of the southern diet. The byproduct of cooked greens is the pot likker. This liquid can be made into a gravy, used as stock for stews and soups, or you can drink it straight up.

The ketogenic diet is a carefully formed strategy that centers around foods that gives a great deal of healthy fats, very low carbohydrates and moderate amounts of protein. The objective is to get a small number of calories from carbohydrates and a bigger number from fats.

The ketogenic diet merges with the southern diet to create an improved diet that underscores high fat and low carb values of the ketogenic diet with the comforting quality of the southern diet. This improved diet highlights the advantages of both diets and positions the dieter to completely harness the advantages of the southern and the ketogenic diet.

Benefits of the Southern Ketogenic diet

The blessings of the southern ketogenic diet are numerous. Several studies have suggested that the ketogenic weight loss plan may additionally help to decrease your vulnerability to coronary illnesses.

Other research has also shown that the ketogenic diet can assist people with type 2 diabetes, insulin resistance and metabolic syndrome. Also, the ketogenic weight loss program distinctly improves nervous system diseases which include Lou Gehrig's, Parkinson's and Alzheimer's sicknesses, and different conditions like PCOS, some kinds of most cancers and zits.

BREAKFAST RECIPES

Delicious Keto Gravy with Sausage

Preparation Time: 5 minutes

Cook Time: 15 minutes

Serve: 8 servings

Ingredients

1/2 tsp fresh ground black pepper

1/2 tsp sea salt

2 cups heavy cream

1 cup low-sodium chicken stock

1/8 tsp flakes red pepper

1 tbsp sage leaves (fresh)

1/2 tsp xanthan gum

1 lb. breakfast sausage (ground)

Preparation

1. On med-high heat, place a big pan over heat.

2. Add in the ground breakfast sausage into the pan and use a spatula to break into smaller pieces.

3. Cook the ground sausage until it is well cooked and browned.

4. Transfer the cooked sausage onto a paper towel to drain the excess fat.

5. Return the drained sausage into the pan and reduce the heat to med-low heat.

6. Season the cooked sausage with xanthan gum and stir together.

7. Add in the red pepper flakes and fresh sage leaves into the sausage mixture.

8. Add in a few tbsps of low-sodium chicken stock per time into the sausage mixture.

9. Stir as you add until a cup of the chicken stock is used.

10. Bring the mixture to simmer on med-heat, stir until a gravy-like consistency is reached.

11. Add in heavy cream into the sausage mixture and stir-cook.

12. Simmer on low-heat until the sausage gravy is thickened as needed.

13. Season with fresh ground black pepper and salt. Stir together.

14. Take off the pan from heat and taste the gravy with sausage to adjust seasoning as needed. Serve with keto biscuits.

Nutritional Information/serving

Calories 396 kcal, Net Carbs 2g, Protein 12g, Dietary Fiber 1g,
Carbohydrates 3g, Fat 38g

Crunchy Almond Flour Cereal with Cinnamon

Preparation Time: 20 minutes

Cook Time: 12 minutes

Serve: 10 servings

Ingredients

1 egg

96g golden erythritol

80g (at room temperature) butter

1/4 tsp kosher salt

1/2 tsp baking soda

1 teaspoon flax meal

2 tsps cinnamon (ground)

192g almond flour

Topping

2 tsps cinnamon (ground)

2 tbsps swerve

28g (melted) butter

Preparation

1. In a medium bowl, add kosher salt, baking soda, flax meal, ground cinnamon and almond flour.

2. Mix the almond flour mixture together until combined and let stand.

3. In a big bowl, add butter and use an electric mixer to beat for 2 minutes to 3 minutes.

4. Add golden erythritol into the beaten butter bowl.

5. Beat butter mixture until a fluffy and light texture is reached.

6. Add egg into the butter mixture and mix until combined.

Note: The butter mixture will not be completely smooth in texture.

7. On low speed, mix the butter mixture and gently add in half of the almond flour mixture. Beat until mixture is combined.

8. Add in the other half of the almond flour mixture into the butter mixture and beat until combined.

9. Use saran wrap to wrap the dough and transfer into a fridge for 1 hour.

10. Place dough between two sheet of parchment paper and roll until a fine thinness is reached. Heat up the oven to 350°F.

11. Slice the dough into small squares using a ruler.

12. On a baking pan, add the parchment paper with the dough, and transfer the baking pan into a refrigerator for 10 minutes.

13. Remove the baking pan from the refrigerator.

14. Brush dough with butter and sprinkle ground cinnamon over the dough. Transfer the dough into the preheated oven.

15. Bake until the dough is completely golden for 8 minutes to 12 minutes.

16. Set aside the almond flour cereal with cinnamon to cool for 10 minutes and place onto a cooling rack.

17. Store in a sealed container and transfer into a fridge for up to 5 days.

Nutritional Information/serving

Calories 172 kcal, Protein 4g, Dietary Fiber 2g, Carbohydrates 4g, Fat 16g

Cheese Shakshuka with Spinach

Preparation Time: 10 minutes

Cook Time: 20 minutes

Serve: 6 servings

Ingredients

4 ounces goat cheese (crumbled)

6 large eggs

3 cups spinach, chopped

1 large (28 ounces) crushed tomatoes, can

1 teaspoon salt

1/2 teaspoon red pepper flakes

1 tablespoon paprika

4 (minced) garlic cloves

1/2 (diced) green bell pepper

1 (minced) jalapeño pepper

1 medium (diced) yellow onion

1/4 cup olive oil

Preparation

1. On med-high heat, place a big cast-iron skillet over heat and add in 1/4 cup of olive oil.

2. Add in minced garlic cloves, diced green bell pepper, minced jalapeno pepper and yellow onion into the skillet.

3. Cook the jalapeno pepper mixture until tender for 3 minutes to 4 minutes.

4. Add paprika, salt and red pepper flakes into the jalapenos pepper mixture. Cook until aromatic for 30 seconds.

5. Add in chopped spinach and tomatoes into the skillet. Cook for 4 minutes to 5 minutes until the spinach wilts.

6. Turn off the heat, make 6 wells in the sauce with a spoon and break egg into each well.

7. Heat up the oven to 425°F.

8. Place the skillet into the oven and bake until the yolks are just runny but the egg whites are cooked for 5 minutes to 10 minutes.

9. Serve with goat cheese.

10. Store in an airtight container and place in the fridge for 72 hours.

Nutritional Information/serving

Calories 248 kcal, Carbohydrates 10.1g, Fat 18.5g, Protein 12.1g, Net Carbs 5.6g

Butter Chocolate Crepes

Preparation Time: 5 minutes

Cook Time: 20 minutes

Serve: 8 servings

Ingredients (crepes)

Ghee

1/2 teaspoon vanilla extract

1/4 teaspoon sea salt

3 teaspoons arrowroot powder

3 tablespoons coconut flour

4 tablespoons coconut oil (melted)

1/2 cup almond milk

6 medium eggs

Chocolate Almond Butter

Salt (a pinch)

6 tablespoons coconut milk

1 teaspoon raw powdered cacao

4 tablespoons almond butter (unsalted & unsweetened)

Preparation

1. In a big mixing bowl, add vanilla extract, salt, arrowroot powder, coconut flour, coconut oil, almond milk and eggs.

2. Whisk the egg mixture until a fine texture is formed. Set mixture aside for 5 minutes.

3. At med-heat, place a heavy bottom skillet over heat and add in a teaspoon of ghee.

4. Reduce heat to med-low heat. Add batter (1/4 cup) into the heated ghee in the skillet.

5. Swirl the skillet to spread the batter and cook the batter until the ends are crispy, for a minute.

6. Turn the crepe and cook for 30 seconds, remove the crepe from the skillet and place on a cooling rack.

7. Repeat the above process with the remaining batter.

8. In a bowl, add in salt, 6 tbsps coconut milk, a tsp of cacao powder and almond butter.

9. Stir the almond butter mixture until a fine texture is reached.

10. Taste the almond butter mixture and add more salt as needed.

11. Serve crepe with chocolate almond butter mixture.

Nutritional Information/serving

Calories 217 kcal, Dietary Fiber 1g, Fat 20.6g, Protein 6g, Carbohydrates 4g

Southern Deviled Eggs

Preparation Time: 10 minutes

Cook Time: 0 minutes

Serve: 12 pieces

Ingredients

Paprika

4–5 tablespoons mayo

1/8 tsp pepper

1/2 tsp dry mustard

1/2 tsp salt

6 eggs (hard cooked), peeled and slice lengthwise in half

Preparation

1. Slice the hard-cooked eggs lengthwise and transfer yolks into a bowl.

2. Use a fork to mash egg yolks.

3. Add in pepper, dry mustard and salt into the mashed egg yolks. Mix together.

4. Add mayo into the egg yolk mixture, a tablespoon per time and mix until a fine texture is formed.

5. Add in the mayo mixture into the halved egg whites until filled.

6. Top the mayo mixture with paprika and serve.

Nutritional Information/Serving

Calories 72 kcal, protein 3.1g, Dietary Fiber 0.2g, Carbohydrates 0.4g, Fat 6.4g

Cinnamon French Toast

Preparation Time: 10 minutes

Cook Time: 10 minutes

Serve: 2 servings

Ingredients

1 tsp vanilla extract

2 tsps stevia

1/3 cup coconut yogurt

1 tbsp ghee

1 coconut flour bread loaf (sliced into 3 evenly pieces)

Garnishes

Edible flowers

Cinnamon

Coconut (shredded)

Fresh berries

Cacao nibs

Preparation

1. On a work surface, place the sliced coconut flour bread and slice each piece into two equal halves.

Note: The bread slices will be 6 in total.

2. At med-heat, place a skillet over heat and add in ghee.

3. Swirl to coat the skillet.

4. Add in two pieces of the sliced bread into the heated ghee and cook until the bread is toasted and golden.

5. Repeat the process above with the remaining bread slices and set aside.

5. In a bowl, add vanilla extract, stevia and coconut yogurt.

6. Beat the coconut yogurt mixture with hand mixer until a just thick texture is formed for a few minutes. Taste and add additional stevia as desired.

7. Serve toasted bread on plates and drizzle extra coconut yoghurt over the bread.

8. Garnish with cacao nibs, berries, cinnamon and edible flowers.

9. Store remaining bread pieces in a sealed container and place in a refrigerator.

Nutritional Information/serving

Calories 683 kcal, Protein 27.9g, Net Carbs 8.9g, Dietary Fiber 8.1g, Carbohydrates 17g, Fat 58g

Chocolate "Oatmeal"

Preparation Time: 5 minutes

Cook Time: 10 minutes

Serve: 2 servings

Ingredients

1 tsp stevia

MitoSweet (a scoop)

1/4 tsp salt

Collagen peptides (a scoop)

1 1/2 tbsps powdered cacao

4 (beaten) eggs

1 cup coconut milk

1 tbsp brain octane oil

2 1/2 cups cauliflower rice

Garnish

Coconut (unsweetened)

cacao nibs

Berries

Preparation

1. On med-heat, place a large saucepan over heat and add a cup of coconut milk. Simmer the coconut milk.

2. Add in the cauliflower rice into the saucepan. Stir until the cauliflower rice is combined with the coconut milk.

3. Adjust heat to low-heat and cook the cauliflower rice for 4 minutes to thicken.

4. Add stevia, salt, mitosweet, collagen peptides, cacao powder and eggs into the saucepan.

5. Lightly stir the cauliflower rice mixture and cook until the eggs is set and well cooked.

6. Stir the chocolate oatmeal and serve.

7. Garnish with berries, unsweetened coconut and cacao nibs as desired.

Nutritional Information/serving

Calories 464.9 kcal, Fat 41.2g, Net Carbs 9.7g, Dietary Fiber 5.3g, Carbohydrates 18g, Protein 22.1g

Egg Sausage Patties

Preparation Time: 10 minutes

Cook Time: 11 minutes

Serve: 1 serving

Ingredients

2 tbsps guacamole

¼ cup water

Fresh black pepper (ground)

Kosher salt

2 large eggs

¼ lb. bulk pork breakfast sausage, raw

3 tbsps ghee, melted

Preparation

1. Use a tablespoon of ghee to grease two (3 1/2") stainless biscuit cutters.

2. On a plate, add the greased biscuit cutters and add in the breakfast sausage.

3. Form a sausage patty by pressing down the breakfast sausage into the biscuit cutters.

4. On med-heat, place a pan over heat and add ghee (1 tbsp).

5. Add in sausage patty into the heated ghee in the pan and cook each side until it is well cooked for 2 minutes to 3 minutes.

6. Transfer the cooked patty onto a plate and set aside.

7. In a small bowl, add in an egg. Crack the second egg into another small bowl and use a fork to pierce the yolks.

8. At med-high heat, place a pan over heat and add a tablespoon of ghee.

9. Transfer the 2 greased biscuit cutters into the heated ghee in the pan and add in the egg.

Note: Pour the egg into a biscuit cutter in the pan and repeat with the second egg.

10. Sprinkle ground black pepper and salt over the egg in each biscuit cutter.

11. Gently add water into the pan with the egg molds avoiding the eggs.

12. Place a tight lid over the pan and reduce the heat to low-heat.

13. Cook the eggs until it is well cooked for 3 minutes.

14. Use a paper towel to line a plate and add the cooked eggs onto the plate.

15. Garnish the eggs in the plate with sausage patties and serve.

Nutritional Information/serving

Calories 783kcal, Dietary Fiber 2g, Fat 73g, Protein 29g, Carbohydrates 3g, Net carb 1g

Coconut Flour Pancakes

Preparation Time: 5 minutes

Cook Time: 10 minutes

Serve: 3 servings

Ingredients

Coconut oil

1/4 tsp Himalayan salt

1/2 cup (unsweetened) almond milk

1/2 cup unsweetened coconut cream

1/2 tsp Ceylon cinnamon

1 tsp vanilla

4 (at room temperature) eggs

2 tbsps (melted) coconut oil

1/2 tsp baking soda

1/2 cup coconut flour

Preparation

1. Add salt, almond milk, coconut cream, Ceylon cinnamon, vanilla, eggs, 2 tbsps of coconut oil, baking soda and coconut flour into an electric blender.

2. Blend the coconut flour mixture until it is well combined.

3. On med-heat, place a medium pan over heat and evenly grease the pan with coconut oil.

4. Scoop 1/2 cup of the almond flour mixture into the greased pan.

5. Cook the dough until a side is golden, turn the pancakes and cook the other side until it is also golden.

6. Transfer the pancake onto a plate and let stand.

7. Repeat the process above with the remaining dough.

8. Serve coconut flour pancakes with berries and grass-fed ghee if desired.

Nutritional Information/serving

Calories 244 kcal, Protein 5.5g, Net Carbs 2.2g, Dietary Fiber 2.7g, Carbohydrates 4.9g, Fat 23g

LUNCH RECIPES

Keto Chicken Lettuce Wraps

Preparation Time: 15 minutes

Cook Time: 1 hour 30 minutes

Serve: 3 servings

Ingredients

Lettuce head

Olive oil

Rice noodle sticks

3 tablespoons soy sauce

2 tablespoons keto brown sugar substitute

1 cup mushrooms (finely diced)

Water chestnuts, small can (finely diced)

3 green onions (finely diced)

3 chicken breasts, boneless skinless (slice into pieces)

Preparation

1. On med-heat, place a big pan over heat and add olive oil (a tbsp).

2. Add in the boneless skinless chicken breasts into the heated oil.

3. Stir-cook the chicken until it is well cooked.

4. Put off the heat, transfer the cooked chicken into a bowl and dice.

5. Add brown sugar and soy sauce into a small bowl, stir together until combined.

6. Add in the diced green onions, water chestnuts, mushrooms and chicken into the pan.

7. Stir in soy sauce mixture to the pan.

8. Stir-cook the chicken mixture on med-heat until it is evenly heated.

9. Line a plate with paper towel.

10. On med-heat, place a small sauce pot over heat and add 2" of olive oil.

11. Heat olive oil for few minutes and add a handful of rice noodle sticks into the heated olive oil.

12. Remove the rice noodle once it is puffed up and transfer onto the prepared plate.

13. On the lettuce leaves, add the chicken with rice noodles. Serve.

Nutritional Information/serving

Calories 449 kcal, Protein 71.3g, Dietary Fiber 1.7g, Carbohydrates 17.5g, Fat 11.6g

Crisped Keto Chicken
Preparation Time: 15 minutes

Cook Time: 1 hour 50 minutes

Serve: 4 servings

Ingredients

1 1/2 cups cider vinegar

1 tsp red pepper flakes (crushed)

1 tbsp hot sauce

3 tbsps keto brown sugar substitute

1 tsp paprika (smoked)

1 tsp black pepper (smoked)

1 tbsp kosher salt

1 whole chicken, skin on bone in

Preparation

1. In a baking dish, add cider vinegar, red pepper flakes, sauce, brown sugar, paprika, black pepper and kosher salt.

2. Stir the cider vinegar mixture together until the brown sugar dissolves.

3. In the baking dish, place the skin side of the chicken down and place a lid over the dish.

4. Heat up the oven to 300°F and transfer the dish into the oven.

5. Bake the chicken for 45 minutes, turn the chicken and bake the other side for another 45 minutes.

6. Remove lid from the dish and set oven to broil.

7. Broil the chicken until the upper part of the chicken is crisped and the skin is golden, for 20 minutes.

8. Transfer the crisped chicken on a plate and sprinkle the cooking juice from the dish over the chicken.

Nutritional Information/serving

Calories 124 kcal, Protein 4.7g, Dietary Fiber 0.5g, Carbohydrates 15.0g, Fat 2.9g

Keto Butter Roasted Chicken

Preparation Time: 15 minutes

Cook Time: 1 hour 30 minutes

Serve: 6 servings

Ingredients

1/2 tsp powdered garlic

1/2 tsp black pepper

1 tsp parsley

1 tsp basil

1 tsp paprika

1 1/2 tsps kosher salt

1/2 cup butter

Vegetables (chopped)

1 (5 pounds) whole chicken

Preparation

1. In a 13 by 9" baking dish, add in 1/2 cup of butter.

2. Heat up the oven to 425°F and place the dish into the oven to melt the butter.

3. Add garlic powder, black pepper, parsley, basil, paprika and kosher salt into a small bowl.

4. Stir the parsley mixture together. Set aside a teaspoon of the mixture in the small bowl.

5. Take baking dish out of the oven and add the whole chicken into the middle of the dish.

6. Use a brush to coat chicken with the melted butter and sprinkle the parsley mixture over the chicken.

7. Add the chopped vegetables into the space around chicken in the dish.

8. Sprinkle the reserved parsley mixture over the veggies.

9. Transfer the baking dish into the oven and bake for 1 hour to 1 hour 30 minutes, without covering the baking dish.

10. Frequently baste the chicken and veggies with the melted butter in the dish, until the chicken is well cooked.

Nutritional Information/serving

Calories 161 kcal, Protein 1.8g, Dietary Fiber 0.7g, Carbohydrates 3.4g, Fat 15.9g

Cheesy Chicken with Lemon

Preparation Time: 10 minutes

Cook Time: 31 minutes

Serve: 4 servings

Ingredients

1/4 tsp basil (dried)

1/2 tsp salt

3 tbsps mayonnaise

1/2 cup parmesan cheese (grated)

1/2 cup (unsalted) butter

1 lime (juice)

3-4 chicken breasts, boneless skinless

Preparation

1. In a zip lock bag, add the boneless skinless chicken breasts and lime juice.

2. Seal the zip lock bag and transfer into a fridge for 1 hour.

Note: Turn the zip lock bag in the fridge at intervals.

3. On med-high heat, place a big pan over heat and add butter (1/4 cup). Heat the unsalted butter until melts.

4. In the pan, add in the lime juice and the marinated chicken breasts.

5. Cook and turn the chicken breasts for 20 minutes until it is golden.

6. Add dried basil, salt, grated parmesan cheese, mayo and the remaining butter into a small bowl.

7. Stir together until it is well combined.

8. On a baking pan, transfer the cooked chicken breasts.

9. Add the parmesan cheese mixture over the chicken breasts and spread.

10. Heat up the oven to 350°F and transfer the baking pan into the oven.

11. Bake the chicken breasts until the parmesan cheese melts for 10 minutes.

Nutritional Information/serving

Calories 350 kcal, Protein 6.4g, Dietary Fiber 0.0g, Carbohydrates 1.8g, Fat 35.5g

Keto Fried Cabbage with Bacon

Preparation Time: 10 minutes

Cook Time: 20 minutes

Serve: 4 servings

Ingredients

Pepper

Salt

1 (chopped) cabbage head

5-6 bacon strips

Preparation

1. Line a plate with paper towels and set aside.

2. Add the bacon strips into a big pan and place the pan over heat.

3. Cook the bacon strips until it is crispy, transfer onto the prepared plate and crumble the cooked bacon.

4. Pour the bacon grease into a bowl, add 2 tbsps of the bacon grease back into the pan and discard the remaining bacon grease.

5. On med-high heat, place the pan with the bacon grease over heat.

6. Add the bacon and cabbage into the pan, stir-cook for 5 minutes.

7. Place a lid over the pan and cook on low-heat for 5 minutes to 10 minutes, until the cabbage is soft as desired.

8. Season fried cabbage with pepper and salt as desired.

Nutritional Information/serving

Calories 112 kcal, Protein 5.2g, Dietary Fiber 0.7g, Carbohydrates 10.4g, Fat 2.9g

Keto Creamy Pork Chops

Preparation Time: 5 minutes

Cook Time: 40 minutes

Serve: 6 servings

Ingredients

Black pepper (ground)

Salt

3 tablespoons ranch seasoning

1/2 cup chicken broth

1/2 cup heavy cream

8 tablespoons butter, salted

8 ounces (softened) cream cheese, slice into 8 pieces

6 pork chops, boneless (thick slice)

Preparation

1. In a bowl, add pork chops, sprinkle ground black pepper and salt over the pork chops.

2. Mix together to coat the pork chops with the seasoning.

3. On med-heat, place a big pan over heat, add in the salted butter (about 4 tablespoons) and cook until melted.

4. Add in the seasoned pork chops into the heated butter, sear each side until it is brown, for 4 minutes to 5 minutes.

5. Adjust heat to med-heat and keep cooking the pork chops until an internal temperature of 135°F.

6. Transfer the cooked pork chops into a bowl and let stand.

7. Add in the chicken broth into the pan and use a spatula to scrape down the golden bits on the side of the pan.

8. Add in heavy cream, 4 tablespoons of butter and the sliced cream cheese into the pan.

9. Stir-cook until a fine texture is reached.

10. Add in 3 tablespoons of ranch seasoning into the cream cheese mixture in the pan. Stir together until combines.

11. Adjust heat to low-heat, add in the set aside cooked pork chops into the pan.

12. Place a lid over pan and bring to a simmer until the creamy pork chops reaches 145°F internal temperature, for 10 minutes.

Nutritional Information/serving

Calories 477 kcal, Dietary Fiber 2g, Fat 39g, Protein 25g, Carbohydrates 2g

Delicious Cauliflower Grits & Shrimp

Preparation Time: 15 minutes

Cook Time: 30 minutes

Serve: 5 servings

Ingredients (cauliflower grits)

2 (sliced) green onions

4 cups rice cauliflower

1 cup (shredded) sharp cheddar cheese

2 tablespoons butter

2 tablespoons tomato paste

1/4 cup heavy cream

1/2 cup almond milk (unsweetened)

Shrimp

1/2 (chopped) bell pepper

1/2 tablespoon (minced) garlic

1 tablespoon butter

4 bacon slices

1 pound large (peeled & deveined) shrimp

2 teaspoons paprika

Salt (a pinch)

1 tablespoon Creole seasoning

Sauce

1/4 cup heavy cream

2 tablespoons cream cheese

1 teaspoon Worcestershire sauce

1/2 cup vegetable broth

Preparation

1. Add shrimp, paprika, salt and Creole seasoning into a small bowl.

2. Toss to coat the shrimp and let stand.

3. Add the bacon slices into a big pan.

4. At med-high heat, place the pan over heat and cook until the bacon is crispy.

5. Transfer the cooked bacon from the pan into a bowl, crumble and let stand.

6. Transfer the bacon bits and pan drippings (2 tablespoons) from the pan into a small bowl.

7. Add in garlic and butter into the pan. Cook the butter mixture for 30 seconds and add in bell pepper.

8. Cook the bell pepper mixture for a minute to 2 minutes until the pepper is just tender.

9. Add in the deveined shrimp into the pan with the pepper mixture.

10. Cook the shrimp mixture for 4 minutes to 5 minutes until the shrimp is cooked.

11. In another bowl, transfer the cooked pepper and shrimp. Let stand.

Note: Don't remove the liquid in the pan.

12. In the pan with the liquid, add in heavy cream, cream cheese, Worcestershire sauce and vegetable broth.

13. Whisk the sauce mixture together to combine.

14. Simmer the sauce mixture until thickened as desired.

15. Add butter, tomato paste, heavy cream and unsweetened almond milk into a big saucepan.

16. Place the saucepan with the almond mixture on low heat and cook the mixture until a low boil is reached.

17. Take the saucepan off heat and add in the cheddar cheese. Stir together until the cheddar cheese melts.

18. Add in the cauliflower rice to the cheese mixture in the saucepan.

19. On low heat, return the saucepan with the cauliflower mixture over heat.

20. Simmer the mixture and stir frequently until the cauliflower is cooked as desired.

21. Serve cauliflower grits and garnish with the sliced green onions, crumbled bacon, sauce and cooked shrimp.

Nutritional Information/Serving

Calories 495 kcal, Dietary Fiber 11.0g, Fat 25.7g, Protein 34.5g, Carbohydrates 20.4g

Keto Chicken Tenders

Preparation Time: 10 minutes

Cook Time: 10 minutes

Serve: 4 servings

Ingredients

Cooking spray

Pepper

Salt

1 teaspoon paprika

1 teaspoon powdered garlic

1 (beaten) egg

1/2 cup coconut flour

1 lb. chicken tenders

Preparation

1. Use a cooking spray to evenly coat an air fryer basket and set aside.

2. In a bowl, add the chicken tenders, sprinkle pepper and salt to season.

3. In a second bowl, add in the beaten egg.

4. In a third bowl, add the coconut flour and set aside.

5. Remove the seasoned chicken tenders from the bowl and immerse it into the coconut flour in the third bowl.

6. Remove tenders from the coconut flour and dip it into the egg in the second bowl.

7. Transfer the chicken tenders back into the coconut flour again to coat.

8. In the sprayed air fryer basket, transfer the coated chicken tenders and cook for 5 minutes at 350°F.

9. Turn the tender in the air fryer basket and cook until an internal temperature of 165°F for 5 minutes.

10. Serve keto chicken tenders.

Nutritional Information/serving

Calories 183 kcal, Protein 25.8g, Dietary Fiber 5.4g, Carbohydrates 9.1g, Fat 3.8g

Southern Keto BLT Wraps

Preparation Time: 15 minutes

Cook Time: 35 minutes

Serve: 4 servings

Ingredients (lettuce Wraps)

1 cup (halved) cherry tomatoes

8 bacon slices (thick)

1 Romaine lettuce, head

Dressing

1/8 tsp powdered onion

1/8 tsp powdered garlic

1/4 tsp pepper

1/4 tsp salt

1 tsp dill (finely chopped)

1 tbsp chives (finely chopped)

1 tbsp parsley (finely chopped)

1 tbsp lemon juice (fresh)

1/4 cup almond milk

1.5 cups mayo

Preparation

1. Use aluminum foil to line a rimmed baking pan.

2. Lay the bacon slices on the prepared baking pan in an even layer.

Note: Leave spaces between bacon slices in the baking pan.

3. Transfer the baking pan into the oven, bake until brown and crisp, for 20 minutes to 35 minutes at 425°F.

4. On paper towels, add on the baked bacon slices to drain fat.

5. In a bowl, add in all the dressing ingredients and stir until combined. Set aside the dressing.

6. On Romaine lettuce leaf, add the baked bacon slices.

7. Add halved cherry tomatoes on the lettuce leaf and dribble the dressing over the bacon slices and tomatoes.

Nutritional Information/serving

Calories 422 kcal, Protein 9g, Dietary Fiber 3g, Carbohydrates 6.4g, Fat 26.9g

Shrimp Scampi

Preparation Time: 14 minutes

Cook Time: 10 minutes

Serve: 2 servings

Ingredients

Salt

1 (zested & sliced into wedges) lime

2 tbsps olive oil

2 medium (spiralized & blotted to remove excess liquid) zucchini

6 (deveined & butterflied) jumbo shrimp, wild-caught

2 tbsps ghee

Garnish

Green onion (sliced)

Flat parsley leaf

Preparation

1. On med-heat, place a big saucepan over heat and add in 2 tablespoons of ghee.

2. Add in the jumbo shrimp into the heated ghee in the saucepan and do not overcrowd.

3. Cook the jumbo shrimp for 2 minutes, flip and cook other side for 2 minutes.

4. Remove cooked shrimps and transfer into a bowl.

5. Repeat the process above with the remaining shrimp.

6. Add in the zucchini into the saucepan and cook until it is tender for 2 minutes.

7. Add in the cooked shrimp back into the saucepan and turn off the heat.

8. Add lime zest and olive oil into the saucepan and stir together.

9. On two plates, share the cooked shrimp, add in lime wedges, sliced green onion and parsley to garnish the shrimp.

10. Sprinkle salt over keto shrimp scampi to season.

Nutritional Information/serving

Calories 335 kcal, Fat 26.1g, Net Carbs 3.6g, Dietary Fiber 2.5g, Carbohydrates 6.1g, Protein 19g

Keto Shrimp Piccata Pasta

Preparation Time: 10 minutes

Cook Time: 20 minutes

Serve: 4 servings

Ingredients

2-3 tbsps capers

1 (thinly sliced) lime

Lime zest (from 1/2 lime)

1/2 cup chicken stock

1/2 cup lime juice

4 tbsps ghee

1 (thinly sliced) shallot

2 (minced) cloves garlic

1/4 tsp powdered garlic

1/2 tsp salt

1 lb. (peeled & deveined) shrimp

2 tbsps ghee

4 (peeled & spiralized) zucchinis

Garnish

Chopped parsley (fresh)

Cracked black pepper (fresh)

Preparation

1. On two layers of paper towels, add spiralized zucchini and lay on another paper towel over the zucchini.

2. Set aside until excess moisture is removed, for 5 minutes.

3. In a bowl, add the deveined shrimp and season with garlic powder and salt.

4. On med-heat, place a big skillet over heat and add in ghee (two tbsps).

5. Heat the ghee and add in seasoned shrimp into the skillet.

6. Cook shrimp until the tails are just curled and the color turns pink, for a minute to 2 minutes per side.

7. Take pan off heat, transfer the cooked shrimp into a bowl and let sit.

8. Add in the sliced shallot and garlic powder into the skillet.

9. Transfer the skillet back to heat, cook until the shallot is just translucent and the garlic is aromatic for 3 minutes.

10. Add in the lime zest, chicken stock and 4 tablespoons of ghee into the skillet.

11. Bring the chicken stock mixture to low boil, add in capers and lime slices into the skillet.

12. Cook until the lime slices are tender, for 4 minutes to 5 minutes.

13. Transfer the reserved zucchini and shrimp into the skillet.

14. Lightly stir to coat, cook until the zucchini is slightly tender and shrimp is warm, for an additional 2 minutes to 3 minutes.

15. Serve keto shrimp piccata pasta and garnish with parsley and black pepper.

Nutritional Information/serving

Calories 431 kcal, protein 29.5g, Dietary Fiber 1.1g, Carbohydrates 6.5g, Fat 24.6

Herbed Bacon Zoodles

Preparation Time: 10 minutes

Cook Time:20 minutes

Serve: 2 servings

Ingredients

Sage fresh leaves (a handful)

¼ cup chicken bone broth

2-3 tablespoons (melted) ghee

Salt

¼–½ teaspoons turmeric

3 cups (zucchini noodles) zoodles

1–1 ½ cups bacon (diced)

2 cups cauliflower

1 cup butternut pumpkin

Preparation

1. Place a saucepan over heat, add in the cauliflower and butternut pumpkin.

2. Steam until the cauliflower and pumpkin are well cooked and tendered. Transfer into a bowl and Set aside.

3. In a pan, add in the bacon and cook until crisped and golden.

4. On a plate, transfer the cooked bacon and leave the bacon fat in the pan.

5. Add in the sage leaves into the pan with the bacon fat and cook until crisp.

6. On the plate with the bacon, add the cooked sage leaves.

7. In the same saucepan used to steamed cauliflower, add in the zucchini noodles and steam until cooked through for a few minutes.

8. In a food processor, add in 2 tablespoons of chicken broth, salt, ghee, turmeric cooked cauliflower and butternut pumpkin.

9. Process the cauliflower mixture until it is creamy and a fine texture is reached.

10. In the food processor with the cauliflower mixture, keep adding a tablespoon of chicken bone broth per time and process until a thick sauce texture is reached.

11. On two plates, divide the cooked zucchini and drizzle the sauce over the zoodles.

12. Top zoodles with sage leaves and the cooked bacon pieces.

13. Season with salt if needed and serve.

Nutritional Information/serving

Calories 397 kcal, Protein 18.5g, Dietary Fiber 7g, Carbohydrates 17.5g, Fat 29.5g

Cream Cauliflower Mash

Preparation Time: 5 minutes

Cook Time: 10 minutes

Serve: 3 servings

Ingredients

1/4 tsp nutmeg

1/4 tsp ginger

1/4 tsp cloves

1/2 tsp cinnamon

Fresh black pepper, ground (a pinch)

Salt (a pinch)

3 tbsps xylitol

2 tbsps heavy cream

3 tbsps butter, unsalted

1/2 cup pumpkin

8 oz cauliflower

Topping

1 tsp butter

2 tbsps xylitol

1/4 cup pecans (chopped)

Preparation

1. In a pan, add little water and cauliflower.

2. Place a lid over the pan and cook cauliflower until it is tender.

3. Drain the cooked cauliflower, transfer into a bowl and set aside.

4. In a food processor, add nutmeg, ginger, cloves, cinnamon, black pepper, salt, heavy cream, unsalted butter, pumpkin and the drained cauliflower.

5. Pulse the cauliflower mixture until a mushy texture is reached.

6. On med-heat, place a cast-iron skillet over heat and add xylitol.

7. Stir-cook until the xylitol is caramelized and let stand to slightly cool, for 1 minute to 2 minutes.

8. In the cauliflower mixture, add in the caramelized xylitol and process until a creamy and fine texture is reached.

Note: Pour the cauliflower into a skillet and cook off some liquid if the mixture is too watery.

9. Transfer the cauliflower mixture into a bowl and let stand.

10. In a small saucepan, add in 2 tablespoons of xylitol and stir-cook until caramelized.

11. Add in 1/4 cup of pecans into the saucepan and stir together until it is evenly coated.

12. Add a teaspoon of butter into the topping mixture and stir together until combined.

13. Set aside the topping mixture to slightly cool.

14. Serve the cream cauliflower mash and top with the pecan mixture and serve.

Nutritional Information/serving

Calories 235 kcal, Dietary Fiber 2g, Fat 23g, Protein 2g, Carbohydrates 7g

Braised Collard Greens with Bacon

Preparation Time: 5 minutes

Cook Time: 45 minutes

Serve: 3 servings

Ingredients

2 bay leaves

1 tbsp balsamic vinegar

2 cups chicken stock

1 1/2 tsps salt

2 large bunches (stem removed & coarsely chopped) collard greens

2 (thinly sliced) shallots

5 (smashed & thinly sliced) cloves garlic

1/2 lb. diced, bacon

Preparation

1. On a med-heat, place a big Dutch oven and add in the diced bacon.

2. Cook the bacon until crisp.

3. On a paper towel, add in the cooked bacon and pat dry.

4. In the Dutch oven, add in the sliced shallots and garlic.

5. Cook the garlic mixture until brown and aromatic for 10 minutes.

6. Add in the bay leaves, balsamic vinegar, chicken stock, salt, cooked bacon and chopped collard greens into the garlic mixture.

7. Stir until combined and place a lid over the Dutch oven. Cook the garlic mixture for 30 minutes.

8. Cook for 10 minutes more uncovered, to reduce the liquid size. Serve.

Nutritional Information/serving

Calories 409 kcal, Protein 18.2g, Dietary Fiber 10.4, Carbohydrates 19.1g, Fat 30.2g

Cheesy Sauce with Broccoli

Preparation Time: 10 minutes

Cook Time: 20 minutes

Serve: 4 servings

Ingredients

1 bag (16 oz) broccoli florets

1/4 tsp black pepper (ground)

1 1/2 tsps salt

1 cup cheddar cheese (shredded)

1/8 cup butter

1 tbsp cornstarch

1 cup milk

Water

Preparation

1. In a small saucepan, add cornstarch and milk. Use a whisker to whisk the milk mixture.

2. On med-heat, place the saucepan over heat and stir-cook until the cornstarch mixture boils.

3. Adjust the heat to low heat and add in butter. Stir together until the butter melts.

4. Add in ground black pepper, salt (1/2 tsp) and shredded cheddar cheese into the saucepan.

5. Stir-cook the sauce until a fine texture is reached and the cheese is melted.

6. Place a lid over the saucepan and let stand.

7. Add water into a saucepan, about 3/4 of the saucepan.

8. Add in a teaspoon of salt into the water in the saucepan.

9. Place the saucepan with the water over med-high heat and bring the water to just boil.

10. Add in the broccoli florets to the saucepan and cook for 4 minutes to 5 minutes, until the broccoli is soft.

11. Drain the cooked broccoli florets and transfer into a bowl.

12. Serve broccoli with the cheese sauce.

Nutritional Information/serving

Calories 231 kcal, Protein 10.6g, Dietary Fiber 0.0g, Carbohydrates 6.3g, Fat 18.0g

Orange Oregano Pulled Pork

Preparation Time: 5 minutes

Cook Time: 8 hours

Serve: 8 servings

Ingredients

1 juiced orange

4 (chopped) garlic cloves

1 (diced) yellow onion

1/2 teaspoon cumin

1 teaspoon pepper

1 teaspoon salt

1 teaspoon oregano

2 tablespoons paprika

4.5 pounds pork shoulder (trim excess fat)

Preparation

1. In a slow cooker, add orange juice, chopped garlic and onion.

2. Add cumin, pepper, salt, oregano and paprika into a small bowl. Mix together until combined.

3. In a big bowl, add the trimmed pork shoulder and season pork with the spice mixture.

4. Transfer the seasoned pork shoulder into the slow cooker with the onion mixture.

5. Cook the pork shoulder for 8 hours on low.

6. On a cutting board, transfer the cooked pork shoulder and shred with two forks.

Nutritional Information/serving

Calories 251 kcal, Dietary Fiber 1g, Fat 11g, Protein 31g, Carbohydrates 4g

Baked Crack Chicken

Preparation Time: 10 minutes

Cook Time: 7 hours

Serve: 10 servings

Ingredients

½ tsp pepper

½ tsp salt

1 tsp red pepper (crushed)

1 tsp dill (dried)

1 tbsp parsley (dried)

1 ½ tsps powdered onion

2 tsps powdered garlic

2 tbsps chives (dried)

1 bunch green onions (chopped)

1 ½ cups cheddar cheese

8 bacon slices

2 (8-Oz) cream cheese

2 lbs. chicken breasts

Preparation

1. In a skillet, add in the 8 bacon slices and fry. Set aside the fried bacon slices.

2. In a slow cooker, add the chicken breasts, pepper, salt, red pepper, dill, parsley, onion powder, garlic powder, chives and cream cheese.

3. Place a lid over the slow cooker and cook on high, for 5 hours and 7 hours on low.

4. Use a fork to shred the cooked chicken breasts.

5. Serve baked crack chicken and top with chopped green onions, fried bacon and cheddar cheese.

6. Store the leftover in an airtight container and place into a freezer for up to 90days.

Nutritional Information/serving

Calories 394 kcal, Protein 28.4g, Dietary Fiber 0.2g, Carbohydrates 3.7g, Fat 29.1g

Spicy Collard Greens with Turkey

Preparation Time: 15 minutes

Cook Time: 1 hour 45 minutes

Serve: 2 servings

Ingredients

Hot sauce

Pepper

Salt

32 ounces (washed thoroughly & slice into strips) collard greens

1 large (cooked) turkey leg, smoked

1 tsp red pepper flakes

3 cups chicken broth

3 cloves (minced) garlic

1 small (finely diced) white onion

1 tbsp olive oil

Preparation

1. At med-heat, place a big and deep pan over heat. Add in a tablespoon of olive oil.

2. Add in the diced white onion into the heated olive oil. Cook the white onion until it is soft.

3. Add in minced garlic into the pan and cook until aromatic.

4. Add in the turkey, red pepper flakes and chicken broth to the pan.

5. Stir and cook until the turkey mixture boils, reduce heat to low heat.

6. Place a lid over pan and lightly boil turkey mixture for 20 minutes to 30 minutes.

7. Take the cooked turkey from the pan and set aside to cool.

8. Separate the bone from the turkey skin and meat.

9. Slice turkey flesh into smaller pieces, transfer the turkey skin and meat back into the pan. Simmer turkey mixture for 10 minutes

10. Add in the sliced collard greens into the pan and press down the collard greens.

11. Cook until the collard greens are just wilted.

12. Place a lid over the pan, bring to simmer and occasionally stir-cook for 60 minutes.

13. Season turkey mixture with pepper and salt as needed.

14. Transfer the cooked collard greens onto a plate, drizzle hot sauce over the collard greens and serve.

Nutritional Information/serving

Calories 692 kcal, Protein 25.0g, Dietary Fiber 12.9g, Carbohydrates 45.5g, Fat 38.9g

Cajun Blackened Fish with Lemon

Preparation Time: 5 minutes

Cook Time: 10 minutes

Serve: 4 servings

Ingredients

2-3 tbsps lemon juice

2 tbsps olive oil

2 tbsps Cajun blackening seasoning

4 (4 oz) catfish fillets

Preparation

1. In a bowl, add in the catfish fillets and sprinkle 2 tablespoons of Cajun blackening seasoning over the fillets.

2. On med-high heat, place a big pan over heat and add 2 tablespoons of olive oil.

3. Add in the seasoned catfish fillets into the heated olive oil and cook for 5 minutes.

4. Flip the catfish fillets and cook for an additional 5 minutes.

5. Serve and sprinkle lemon juice over the cooked catfish.

Nutritional Information/serving

Calories 316 kcal, Protein 16.1g, Dietary Fiber 4.0g, Carbohydrates 14.8g, Fat 22.8g

Keto Crab Bisque

Preparation Time: minutes 10 minutes

Cook Time: 10 minutes

Serve: 8 servings

Ingredients

1/4 teaspoon white pepper

1/8 tsp cayenne pepper

1/2 tsp salt

2 cups coconut milk

3 cups vegetable stock

1 (diced) red bell pepper

3 (minced) garlic cloves

1 small (diced) onion

1 tablespoon coconut oil

1 pound lump crab meat

Preparation

1. Add a tablespoon of coconut oil into a medium size pot and place the pot over heat.

2. Add in the minced garlic and diced onions into the heated coconut oil.

3. Cook the onion mixture until the onions are translucent.

4. Add the diced red bell pepper into the onion mixture and cook for a minute to 2 minutes.

5. Add white pepper and cayenne pepper into the onion mixture. Sprinkle salt to taste.

6. Add a tablespoon of coconut milk into the pot.

7. Cook on low heat and simmer, for 2 minutes to 3 minutes.

8. Stir in the vegetable stock to the onion mixture and bring to simmer again.

9. Fold in the lump crab meat and cook until it is warm.

Nutritional Information/serving

Calories 158 kcal, Protein 11g, Carbohydrates 4g, Fat 11g

Smoked Chicken Salad

Preparation Time: 10 minutes

Cook Time: 0 minutes

Serve: 4 servings

Ingredients (seasonings)

Pepper (a pinch)

Salt (a pinch)

1/2 teaspoon powdered cayenne

1 teaspoon sweetener

1 teaspoon paprika

1 teaspoon powdered onion

1 teaspoon powdered garlic

Chicken

1 (diced) green onion

2 stalks (diced) celery

1/2 teaspoon liquid smoke

1 tablespoon mustard

1/2 cup mayonnaise

1 shredded rotisserie chicken

Preparation

1. Add liquid smoke, mustard and mayonnaise into a medium bowl. Whisk the mayonnaise mixture together.

2. Add in the desired seasoning into the mayonnaise mixture and whisk until combined.

3. Add in diced green onions, celery and shredded rotisserie chicken into the mayo mixture. Stir together until combined.

4. Serve the smoked chicken salad.

Nutritional Information/serving

Calories 257 kcal, Protein 21g, Dietary Fiber 1g, Net Carbs 1g, Carbohydrates 2g, Fat 18g

Seared Marinated Chicken

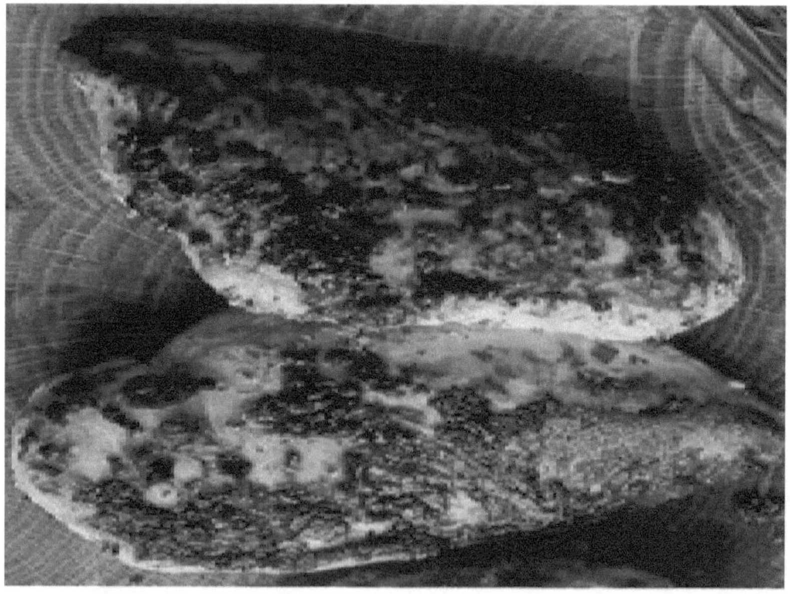

Preparation Time: 10 minutes

Cook Time: 20 minutes

Serve: 6 servings

Ingredients

A bottle marinade dressing

6 chicken breast, boneless skinless

Vegetable oil

Preparation

1. In a big ziplock bag, add in the boneless skinless chicken breasts.

2. Add in the marinade dressing over the chicken breasts in the ziplock bag.

3. Seal the ziplock bag and transfer into a fridge for 8 hours.

4. Grease a pan with vegetable oil.

5. On med-high heat, place the greased pan over heat.

6. Add the marinated chicken breasts into the heated pan.

7. Cook the chicken breasts for 10 minutes, turn and cook until the chicken breasts are no longer pink in the middle and well cooked.

8. Serve seared marinated chicken.

Nutritional Information/serving

Calories 372 kcal, Protein 69.3g, Dietary Fiber 0.0g, Carbohydrates 1.3g, Fat 9.8g

DINNER RECIPES

Keto Smoky BBQ Ribs

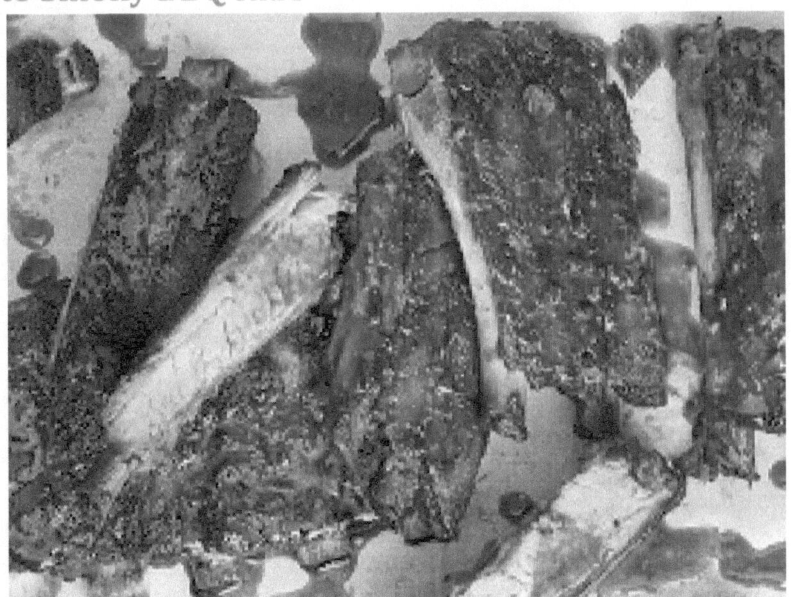

Preparation Time: 10 minutes

Cook Time: 8 hours 10 minutes

Serve: 3 servings

Ingredients

1/4 teaspoon powdered stevia

2 cloves garlic (minced)

1/2 teaspoon black pepper

1/2 teaspoon salt

1/2 teaspoon cayenne pepper

1 tablespoon liquid smoke

1 tablespoon paprika (smoked)

1 tablespoon Worcestershire sauce

1/2 cup tomatoes (crushed)

BBQ Sauce (sugar free)

38 ounces rack spare ribs

Preparation

1. Add BBQ sauce and garlic into a bowl, mix until the sauce mixture combines.

2. In a slow cooker, add in BBQ sauce and rack spare ribs.

3. Place the slow cooker over heat and cook the rack spare ribs mixture for 4 hours on high or 8 hours on low.

4. Heat up the oven to 410°F.

5. Gently transfer the cooked rib from the slow cooker onto a baking sheet.

6. Drizzle BBQ sauce (1/2 tablespoon) from the slow cooker over the ribs on the baking sheet.

7. Transfer the baking sheet into the preheated oven and roast ribs until crisp for 10 minutes.

8. In a bowl, transfer the remaining BBQ sauce from the slow cooker.

9. Remove the baking sheet from the oven and slice the ribs.

10. Dip the ribs in the remaining BBQ sauce and serve.

Nutritional Information/Serving

Calories 804 kcal, Net Carbs 3.63g, Protein 46.37g, Dietary Fiber 0.7g, Carbohydrates 4.33g, Fat 62.94g

Creamy Sausage Gravy and Keto Chicken Fried Steak

Preparation Time: 15 minutes

Cook Time: 20 minutes

Serve: 4 servings

Ingredients (chicken fried steak)

Cooking oil

Cayenne pepper (a pinch)

1 teaspoon paprika

1 1/2 teaspoons powdered garlic

1 1/2 teaspoons powdered onion

1/2 cup (grated) parmesan cheese

1 1/2 cups pork rinds (crushed)

2 large eggs

1/4 cup heavy cream

Black pepper

Salt

1 pound (pounded to 1/4" thick) steak cubes

Creamy sausage gravy

1/2 teaspoon salt

1 tablespoon (chopped) parsley, fresh

1 1/2 cups heavy cream

3 cloves (minced) garlic

2/3 cup (diced) onion

12 ounces pork sausage links (sliced)

2 tablespoons butter

Preparation

1. In a bowl, add in the steak cubes, season both sides with black pepper and salt.

2. Add eggs and heavy cream into a flat bottom bowl.

3. Whisk the heavy cream mixture together and set aside.

4. Add in the cayenne pepper, paprika, garlic powder, onion powder, parmesan cheese and pork rinds into a bowl. Stir together.

5. On med-high heat, place a big heavy bottom skillet over heat.

6. Add in 1/4" to 1/2" of cooking oil into the skillet.

7. Dredge the seasoned cube steaks into the heavy cream mixture, remove and transfer each into the pork rinds mixture.

8. Thoroughly coat both sides of the cube steaks with the pork rinds mixture.

9. In the heated cooking oil, add the breaded cube steak.

10. Fry each side for 3 minutes until the breaded steak is golden and crispy.

11. On med-heat, place a big skillet over heat and add in 2 tbsps of butter.

12. Add in the pork sausage links into the heated butter.

13. Cook the pork sausage until it is golden.

14. Transfer the pork sausage into a bowl with a slotted spoon and leave the pan drippings in the skillet.

15. Add in minced garlic and diced onion into the drippings in the skillet.

16. Reduce the heat to med-low, stir-cook the diced onion until it is tender and translucent.

17. Add in salt, parsley and heavy cream into the skillet.

18. Adjust the heat to med-heat and cook the heavy cream mixture until just boiling. Simmer until the gravy thickens on low-heat.

19. Add in the cooked pork sausage into the skillet.

20. Serve chicken fried steak and top with the sausage gravy.

Nutritional Information/serving

Calories 1,254 kcal, Protein 76.9, Dietary Fiber 13.0g, Carbohydrates 12.8, Fat 105.5g

Creamy Cauliflower Broccoli Casserole with Chicken

Preparation Time: 10 minutes

Cook Time: 35 minutes

Serve: 6 servings

Ingredients

3 ounces cheddar cheese (shredded)

1/4 tsp powdered onion

1/4 tsp powdered garlic

1/8 tsp pepper

1/4 tsp salt

2 tbsps parmesan cheese

2 tbsps olive oil

2 cups (cooked & chopped) chicken breasts

2 cups cauliflower, florets

3 cups florets, broccoli

Preparation

1. Heat up the oven to 400°F. Add cauliflower florets into a pot.

2. Add in water to cover the cauliflower florets in the pot.

3. Cook cauliflower until it is fork-tender. Strain the cauliflower florets and leave the cooking juice in the pot.

4. Add the broccoli florets into a big bowl and place into the microwave for 4 minutes.

5. Take broccoli bowl out of the microwave and add in the chopped chicken breasts.

6. In an electric blender, add salt, pepper, garlic powder, onion powder, parmesan cheese, olive oil and the cooked cauliflower.

7. Blend the cauliflower mixture until a fine texture is formed.

Note: If the sauce is too thick, add the reserved cauliflower juice to thin out.

8. Add the sauce into the bowl with the broccoli florets.

9. Mix the sauce with the broccoli and chopped chicken breast.

10. In a baking dish, transfer the coated broccoli florets and chicken.

11. Add the cheddar cheese over the chicken broccoli florets and place into the preheated oven.

12. Bake chicken broccoli florets for 20 minutes and serve.

Nutritional Information/serving

Calories 126 kcal, Protein 5.6g, Dietary Fiber 0.4g, Carbohydrates 2.8g, Fat 10.0g

Pepperoncini Pot Roast

Preparation Time: 5 minutes

Cook Time: 8 hours

Serve: 8 servings

Ingredients

1 jar (drain) pepperoncini peppers

1 stick butter, salted

1 (1 ounce) onion soup mix, packet

1 (1 ounce) packet ranch dressing mix

3–4 lb. roasted beef chuck

Preparation

1. In a slow cooker, add in the roasted beef chuck.

2. Sprinkle the onion soup mix and ranch dressing mix over the roasted beef chuck.

3. Add in the drained pepperoncini peppers and butter over the roast.

4. Cook pepperoni pot roast for 6 hours to 8 hours on low.

Nutritional Information/serving

Calories 332 kcal, Protein 34.3g, Carbohydrates 0.6g, Fat 21.8g

Taco Soup with Chicken

Preparation Time: 10 minutes

Cook Time: 4 hours

Serve: 8 servings

Ingredients

½ tbsp lime juice

3 tbsps lemon juice

¼ tsp salt

1 tsp paprika

1 tsp chili powder

1.5 tbsps cumin

½ cup (diced) onion

4 (minced) garlic cloves

2 (8 oz) cream cheese, packs

2 (10 oz) rotel tomatoes, cans

4 cups chicken broth

2 lbs. chicken thighs (thawed)

Toppings

Sour Cream

Tomatoes (diced)

Jalapenos, sliced

Green onions

Cheddar cheese

Preparation

1. In a slow cooker, add the chicken thighs, lime juice, lemon juice, salt, paprika, chili powder, cumin, minced garlic and diced onion.

2. Add in the tomatoes and chicken broth into the chicken thigh mixture.

3. Cook the chicken for 4 hours on high.

4. Transfer the cooked chicken thighs into a bowl and shred.

5. Add the shredded chicken back into the slow cooker and add in cream cheese.

6. Stir the soup together and serve.

7. Store remaining taco soup with chicken in a sealed container and place into a freezer for 90 days.

Note: You can add the cream cheese into the soup when it thawed rather than adding it into the slow cooker.

Nutritional Information/serving

Calories 360 kcal, Protein 30.6g, Dietary Fiber 1.5g, Carbohydrates 7.5g, Fat 23.1g

Keto Southern Style Lasagna

Preparation Time: 30 minutes

Cook Time: 1 hour

Serve: 4 servings

Ingredients (noodles)

1/4 teaspoon powdered onion

1/4 teaspoon powdered garlic

1/4 teaspoon Italian seasoning

1 1/4 cup (shredded) mozzarella cheese

1/4 cup (grated) parmesan cheese

4 ounces softened, cream cheese

2 large eggs

Filling

1 teaspoon Italian seasoning

1 teaspoon basil (dried)

1 teaspoon powdered garlic

1 teaspoon oregano (dried)

1 tablespoon onion flakes (minced)

6 tablespoons milk ricotta cheese, whole

3/4 cup (shredded) mozzarella cheese

1 1/2 cups (divided) three cheese marinara sauce

1 pound beef, ground

Salt (a pinch)

Preparation

1. Use parchment paper to line a baking dish of 13 by 9" and heat up the oven to 375°F.

2. Add eggs and softened cream cheese into a big bowl. Whisk together with a hand mixer.

3. Add in onion powder, garlic powder, Italian seasoning and grated parmesan cheese into the cream cheese mixture.

4. Stir cream cheese mixture together until combined.

5. Gently fold in the shredded mozzarella cheese with a rubber spatula into the cream cheese mixture.

6. Stir together until the mixture combined.

7. In the lined baking dish, transfer the cream cheese mixture and spread.

8. Form even layer with the cream cheese mixture in the baking dish.

9. Place the baking dish on the center rack of the oven and bake noodles for 20 minutes to 25 minutes.

10. Transfer the baking dish into a refrigerator for 20 minutes to cool the noodles. Slice the noodles into three even size.

11. On med-high heat, place a big pan over heat.

12. Add in salt, basil, garlic powder, dried oregano, onion and ground beef into the pan.

13. Cook the ground beef mixture until the beef is golden.

14. Drain the cooked ground beef to remove excess fat and move cooked beef to a plate.

15. Add in marinara sauce (3/4 cup) into the pan, simmer mixture for 10 minutes on low heat. Divide the beef mixture into 3 equal portions.

16. In a loaf pan, add in the remaining marinara sauce to the base of the loaf pan.

17. Add in the first layer of the noodles over the marinara sauce in the loaf pan.

18. Add a portion of the beef mixture over the noodles and garnish with ricotta cheese (three tablespoons) and mozzarella cheese (1/4 cup).

19. Add the second layer of the noodles over the mozzarella cheese.

20. Repeat the above assembling-process with the remaining layers of the noodles, ground beef, ricotta and mozzarella cheese.

21. Season the top with Italian seasoning.

22. Transfer the loaf pan into the oven and bake for 20 minutes.

Nutritional Information/serving

Calories 654 kcal, Protein 48.2g, Dietary Fiber 2.9g, Fat 43.6g, Carbohydrates 16.9g

Bacon Chicken Jalapeno Popper

Preparation Time: 10 minutes

Cook Time: 35 minutes

Serve: 8 servings

Ingredients

Salt

Pepper

1 clove garlic

1/4 cup chicken stock

1 cup heavy cream

1 cup cheddar cheese (shredded)

8 oz cream cheese

4 jalapeno peppers (rinsed, sliced & removed seeds)

5 bacon, slices (fried and crumbled)

6 chicken breasts

Preparation

1. Heat up the oven to 375°F.

2. In a pot, add in the chicken breast and cook until the chicken is soft.

3. Transfer the chicken breast into a bowl and shred.

4. Add garlic clove, heavy cream, chicken stock and cream cheese into a mixing bowl.

5. Stir the heavy cream mixture together until combined.

6. Sprinkle pepper and salt over the heavy cream mixture as desired.

7. Add the shredded chicken breasts into a casserole dish, top with the heavy cream mixture and jalapenos peppers.

8. Garnish with bacon slices and shredded cheddar cheese.

9. Transfer the casserole dish into the oven and bake for 20 minutes.

10. Serve bacon chicken jalapenos popper.

Nutritional Information/serving

Calories 286 kcal, Protein 12.5g, Dietary Fiber 0.2g, Carbohydrates 3.3g, Fat 24.8g

Southern Beefy casserole

Preparation Time: 15 minutes

Cook Time: 30 minutes

Serve: 10 servings

Ingredients

Pepper

Salt

Tomatoes (diced)

Lettuce (shredded)

Dill pickles

6 (fried and crumbled) bacon slices

4 cups cheddar cheese

2 tsps Worcestershire sauce

2 tbsps yellow mustard

4 cloves (minced) garlic

1 cup onion (diced)

1 cup heavy cream

4 eggs

4 oz cream cheese

2 lbs. beef, ground

Preparation

1. Grease a casserole dish and heat up the oven to 350°F.

2. In a medium bowl, add in the yellow mustard, heavy cream, cheddar cheese (two cups) and eggs. Stir until combined.

3. In a bowl, add the crumbled bacon slices and let stand.

4. In a pan, add in the ground beef, cook until the beef is brown.

5. Add in pepper, salt, Worcestershire sauce, minced garlic and onion into the pan with the beef.

6. Cook the ground beef mixture until it is brown. Drain and discard the fat in the pan.

7. Add in the cream cheese over the beef mixture.

8. Transfer the beef mixture into the prepared casserole dish.

9. Add in dill pickles, two cups of cheddar cheese, crumbled bacon and heavy cream mixture over the ground beef mixture.

10. Place the casserole dish into the oven and bake for 20 minutes.

11. Serve Southern beefy casserole, garnish with diced tomatoes and lettuce.

Nutritional Information/serving

Calories 517 kcal, Protein 38.3g, Dietary Fiber 0.3g, Carbohydrates 3.9g, Fat 38.1g

Herbed Chicken Bake

Preparation Time: 10 minutes

Cook Time: 40 minutes

Serve: 12 servings

Ingredients

3 tablespoons Dijon mustard

2 ounces mayo

1 egg

12 medium size bone-in chicken skinless thighs and legs

1 teaspoon dried paprika smoked

0.5 teaspoon dried garlic powder

1 teaspoon (dried) oregano

1 teaspoon (dried) black pepper

1 teaspoon salt

1.5 teaspoon (dried) thyme

4 ounces pork rinds

Preparation

1. Heat up the oven to 400°F.

2. In a bowl, add and crush the pork rinds until a fine-coarse consistency is formed.

3. Add in paprika, garlic powder, dried oregano, dried black pepper, salt and dried thyme into the pork rind bowl.

4. Stir the pork rind mixture together and transfer onto a flat dish. Spread the mixture in a thin layer.

5. Add Dijon mustard, mayonnaise and egg into a wide bowl. Stir together.

6. Dip each chicken thigh and leg into the mayonnaise mixture.

7. Transfer each coated chicken into the pork rind mixture.

8. Roll the chicken in pork rinds mixture until the chicken coats evenly.

9. In a baking sheet, place a wire rack and top with the coated chicken.

10. Transfer the baking sheet into the oven and bake herbed chicken for 40 minutes.

Nutritional Information/serving

Calories 308.25 kcal, Dietary Fiber 0.26g, Fat 14.79g, Protein 40.4g, Carbohydrates 0.73g, Net Carbs 0.47g

Turkey Keto Chili

Preparation Time: 5 minutes

Cook Time: 10 minutes

Serve: 4 servings

Ingredients

Pepper

Salt

1/2 cup salsa

1/2 teaspoon powdered garlic

1 teaspoon coriander, ground

1 teaspoon cumin, ground

1 pound lean turkey, ground

Preparation

1. Add pepper, salt, garlic, coriander, cumin and ground turkey into a medium saucepan.

2. On med-heat, place the saucepan over heat and cook the ground turkey mixture for 5 minutes.

3. Add in the salsa into the saucepan when the turkey is well cooked.

4. Simmer turkey mixture for 5 minutes on low heat.

5. Serve turkey and garnish with sour cream, avocado and red onion.

Nutritional Information/serving

Calories 200 kcal, Protein 20.2g, Dietary Fiber 0.4g, Carbohydrates 6.9g, Fat 9.1g

Cheese Chicken Pot Pie

Preparation Time: 20 minutes

Cook Time: 30 minutes

Serve: 8 servings

Ingredients (crust)

1 1/2 teaspoons parsley (dried)

1/3 cup (grated) mozzarella cheese

1 cup (grated) cheddar cheese

1/4 tsp baking powder

1/4 tsp salt

4 eggs

2 tbsps sour cream

1/3 cup coconut flour

4 1/2 tbsps melted butter

Filling

1/4 teaspoon Xanthan Gum

2 1/2 cups chicken (cooked & diced)

Thyme (a pinch)

1/4 teaspoon rosemary

1 teaspoon poultry seasoning

1 cup chicken broth

3/4 cup heavy cream, whipping

2 (minced) garlic cloves

1/4 teaspoon pepper

1/4 teaspoon pink salt

1/4 small (diced) onion

1/2 cup green beans

2 tbsps butter

Preparation

1. Heat up the oven to 400°F.

2. In an oven proof dish, add pepper, pink salt, minced garlic cloves, green beans and diced onion.

3. Cook the green beans mixture until the onion is translucent for 5 minutes.

4. Add in rosemary, thyme, poultry seasoning, chicken broth and heavy cream into the green bean mixture.

5. Sprinkle 1/4 teaspoon of xanthan gum over the green bean mixture. Stir together.

6. Place a lid over the oven proof dish over stove top and simmer sauce mixture to thicken for 5 minutes.

7. Add in the chicken into the sauce.

8. In a bowl, add sour cream, salt, eggs and butter. Whisk the butter mixture together.

9. Add in baking powder and coconut flour into the butter mixture.

10. Stir the butter mixture together until combined.

11. Add in the grated mozzarella cheese and cheddar cheese into the butter mixture. Stir together.

12. In the oven proof dish, add the batter, in dollops.

Note: Don't spread the batter in the dish.

13. Transfer the oven dish into the preheated oven and bake for 15 minutes to 20 minutes.

14. Place cheese chicken pot pie under broiler and boil until the cheeses are brown, for a minute to 2 minutes.

15. Serve and top the cheese chicken pot pie with dried parsley.

Nutritional Information/serving

Calories 297 kcal, Dietary Fiber 2g, Fat 17g, Protein 11.6g, Carbohydrates 5.3g

Pork Keto Mac and Cheese

Preparation Time: 5 minutes

Cook Time: 10 minutes

Serve: 8 servings

Ingredients

1 tbsp olive oil

White pepper, ground

Chopped parsley

1/3 cup (crushed) pork rinds

1 cup (grated) mozzarella cheese

1 ½ cups pulled pork (divided)

1 ½ cups creamy cheese sauce

1 (cut in florets) cauliflower head

Preparation

1. Place a pot over heat and add in water.

2. Bring the water to boil and add in the cauliflower.

3. Place a lid over the pot and cook cauliflower florets for a minute to 2 minutes.

4. In a bowl, add in ice water and transfer the cooked cauliflower into the bowl, for 3 minutes to 5 minutes.

5. Remove the cauliflower, get rid of the excess water.

6. On a plate, transfer the cooked cauliflower.

7. On low heat, place a big pan over heat and add in olive oil and creamy cheese sauce.

8. Cook the creamy cheese sauce until it is well cooked.

9. Add in the cooked cauliflower and grated mozzarella cheese into the pan.

10. Add in the white pepper to the creamy cheese sauce mixture.

11. Stir the creamy cheese sauce mixture together until combined and cook until the mozzarella cheese is melted.

12. Add in the pulled pork (1 1/4 cups) into the pan and stir together.

13. On a serving plate, transfer the pork mixture and top with chopped parsley and 1/4 cup of pulled pork and pork rinds.

Nutritional Information/serving

Calories 221 kcal, Dietary Fiber 1g, Fat 15g, Protein 14g, Carbohydrates 8g

Creamy Taco Casserole

Preparation Time: 5 minutes

Cook Time: 40 minutes

Serve: 6 servings

Ingredients

1/2 cup pepper jack cheese (grated)

1/2 cup cheddar cheese (grated)

1/4 cup heavy cream

1 tbsp hot sauce

4 eggs

1/4 cup salsa

2 oz cream cheese

1/4 cup water

1 packet taco seasoning

1 minced jalapeno

1/4 cup onion (chopped)

1 lb. beef, ground

Preparation

1. Use non-stick spray to coat a baking dish of 8 by 8" and heat up the oven to 350°F.

2. On med-heat, place a big pan over heat and add in the ground beef into the pan.

3. Cook the ground beef until it is brown.

4. Add in minced jalapeno and chopped onion into the pan.

5. Cook until the chopped onion is just translucent and get rid of the grease.

6. Add in 1/4 cup of water and taco seasoning into the pan.

7. Stir and cook the beef mixture for about 5 minutes.

8. Add in the salsa and grated cream cheese into the beef mixture. Stir together until combined.

9. In a medium bowl, add in the heavy cream, hot sauce and eggs. Whisk together until combined.

10. In the sprayed baking dish, transfer the beef mixture and pour egg mixture over the beef mixture.

11. Sprinkle grated pepperjack cheese and cheddar cheese over the egg mixture.

12. Transfer the baking dish into the oven and bake until the egg is well cooked for 30 minutes.

13. Set aside the baking dish for 5 minutes to cool.

14. Slice creamy taco casserole and serve.

Nutritional Information/serving

Calories 406 kcal, Dietary Fiber 1g, Fat 28g, Protein 30g, Carbohydrates 5g

Cheesy Cauliflower Caprese Casserole

Preparation Time: 15 minutes

Cook Time: 1 hour 15 minutes

Serve: 6 servings

Ingredients

1/3 tsp black pepper, ground (divided)

¼ tsp salt (divided)

Chopped basil leaves (a handful)

1 cup (halved) grape tomatoes

1 cup mozzarella cheese (shredded)

1/3 cup parmesan cheese (grated)

1/3 cup heavy cream

2 tbsps tomato paste

1 cup tomato sauce

1 medium (cut into florets) cauliflower head

Olive oil

Preparation

1. Use a little olive oil to rub a med-large baking dish. Let stand.

2. Place a rack in the middle of the oven and heat up the oven to 425°F.

3. In a high-sided baking pan, add the cauliflower florets and arrange in an even layer.

4. Sprinkle ground black pepper, salt and olive oil (1 tbsp) over the layered cauliflower florets.

5. Transfer the baking pan into the oven and bake until the florets are caramelized lightly, for 30 minutes.

6. On low heat, place a big saucepan over heat and add in tomato paste and sauce. Cook until the tomato mixture is warm.

7. Add in ground black pepper, salt, grated parmesan cheese and heavy cream into the tomato mixture.

8. Stir the tomato mixture until combined.

9. Turn off the heat and add in the baked cauliflower florets into the tomato mixture. Stir together.

10. Add in basil (a pinch), half of grape tomatoes and 1/2 cup of shredded mozzarella cheese into the tomato mixture.

11. In the greased baking dish, transfer cauliflower mixture.

12. Sprinkle 1/2 cup of mozzarella cheese over the cauliflower mixture.

13. Add the remaining half of the grape tomatoes over the cauliflower mixture.

14. Reduce the oven heat to 350°F and transfer the baking dish into the oven.

15. Bake the cauliflower mixture for 30 minutes and broil until the mozzarella cheese releases bubbles and is golden, for a minute to 2 minutes.

16. Remove the baking dish from the oven and set aside for 5 minutes to cool.

17. Sprinkle the remaining basil leaves over the cauliflower casserole.

18. Serve the cheesy cauliflower caprese casserole.

Nutritional Information/serving

Calories 178 kcal, Protein 9g, Carbohydrates 12g, Fat 10g

Southern Fried Chicken

Preparation Time: 20 minutes

Cook Time: 7 minutes

Serve: 6 servings

Ingredients

1/2 cup parmesan (powdered)

1/2 cup almond meal

2 tablespoons heavy Cream

1 egg

1 teaspoon oregano (dried)

1/2 teaspoon powdered chilli (hot)

2 teaspoons. celery salt

1 teaspoon powdered garlic

2 lbs. fillets chicken thigh (sliced each into three evenly pieces)

Preparation

1. In a bowl, add in the sliced fillets chicken thigh.

2. Add in oregano, chilli powder, salt and garlic powder into the chicken bowl.

3. Mix the salt mixture together. Evenly coat the sliced chicken with celery salt mixture.

4. Set aside the coated chicken for 30 minutes to marinate.

5. In another bowl, add in the heavy cream and egg. Whisk together until combined.

6. In a third bowl, add in parmesan and almond meal. Mix and transfer almond mixture onto a tray.

7. Heat up a deep fryer to 180°C.

8. Immerse each chicken piece into the heavy cream mixture and transfer into the almond meal mixture in the tray.

9. Let the coated chicken pieces stand in the tray.

10. Transfer the coated chicken pieces into the deep fryer and do not overcrowd.

Note: If the deep fryer is too small fry the chicken pieces in batches to prevent overcrowding.

11. Fry the chicken pieces until it is brown for 5 minutes to 7 minutes and serve.

Nutritional Information/serving

Calories 359 kcal, Dietary Fiber 0g, Fat 18g, Protein 44g, Carbohydrates 1g

Mustard Herb Crusted Ham Bake

Preparation Time: 10 minutes

Cook Time: 45 minutes

Serve: 6 servings

Ingredients

1/2 cup water

3 pounds ham, smoked

Fresh pepper (ground)

2 tablespoons (chopped) rosemary

2 tablespoons (minced) garlic

1/2 cup mayo

1 cup mustard

Garnish

Cauliflower mash

Roasted asparagus

Preparation

1. In a small bowl, add in smoked ham, pepper, rosemary, garlic, mayo and mustard.

2. In a roasting pan, add the ham with the fat side facing up

3. Liberally coat ham with the mustard mixture in the small bowl.

4. Heat up the oven to 300°F.

5. Add water to the base of the roasting pan and transfer the pan into the prepared oven.

6. Bake the coated ham for 45 minutes without covering the pan.

7. Serve herb crusted ham bake with cauliflower mash and asparagus as desired.

Nutritional Information/serving

Calories 431 kcal, Protein 38.5, Dietary Fiber 2.7g, Carbohydrates 12.8g, Fat 21.1g

Shirataki Noodles with Shrimp Pad Thai

Preparation Time: 15 minutes

Cook Time: 6 minutes

Serve: 3 servings

Ingredients

Sea salt

2 (chopped) green onions

¼ cup cilantro

¼ tsp red pepper(crushed)

1 (minced) garlic clove

1 tsp cashew butter

1 (juiced & divided) lime

2 tbsps coconut aminos

1 ½ tbsps (divided) brain octane oil

2 beaten eggs

18 medium shrimp, wild-caught

2 (7-oz) packages shirataki noodles

Preparation

1. In a bowl, add in the shirataki noodles and rinse noodles for 15 seconds.

2. In a pot, add in water and the rinsed shirataki noodles.

3. Boil noodles for 2 minutes, drain the moisture and transfer noodles into pan.

Note: Don't grease the pan.

4. On med-heat, place the pan with the noodles over heat. For a minute, dry roast the noodles and let stand.

5. Add red pepper, garlic clove, cashew butter, half of the lime juice, coconut aminos and brain octane oil (3/4 tbsp) into a small bowl.

6. Mix together and let stand.

7. On med-heat, place a big pan over heat and add in salt (a pinch), wild-caught shrimp and the remaining brain octane oil.

8. Cook shrimp mixture on each side, for 1 minute 30 seconds to 2 minutes.

9. Shift the cooked shrimp to a side of the pan and add in the egg into the free side of the pan.

10. Cook the egg immediately for a minute until a tender scramble is reached.

11. Add in the chopped green onions, cilantro, coconut aminos mixture and the cooked shirataki noodles into the pan with the eggs.

12. Toss the noodles mixture to coat and stir until combined. Heat the mixture until it is warm.

13. Top the noodles mixture in the pan with the remaining half of the lime juice.

14. Taste, add more red pepper and salt as needed.

Nutritional Information/serving

Calories 180 kcal, Fat 12g, Net Carbs 5g, Dietary Fiber 0g, Carbohydrates 5g, Protein 12g

Cheese Meatball Casserole

Preparation Time: 15 minutes

Cook Time: 45 minutes

Serve: 8 servings

Ingredients (meatball)

1 teaspoon salt

2 teaspoons basil, dried

2 teaspoons (minced) dried garlic

2 teaspoons (minced) dried onion

1 egg

1 cup spinach (chopped)

1/3 cup parmesan cheese (grated)

1 cup mozzarella cheese (shredded)

1 pound Italian pork sausage

1 pound chicken, ground

Casserole

8 ounces cheese (shredded)

1 cup pasta sauce (sugar free)

Preparation

1. Use cooking spray to spray a casserole dish and heat up the oven to 400°F.

2. In a bowl, add salt, basil, minced garlic, onion, egg, spinach, parmesan cheese, mozzarella cheese, Italian pork sausage and ground chicken.

3. Mix the chicken mixture until combined.

4. Cut and roll out 24 meatballs. Transfer the meatballs into the sprayed casserole dish.

5. Place the casserole dish into the oven and bake the meatballs until well-cooked for 30 minutes.

6. Remove the dish from the oven and gently drain the meatballs grease from the dish.

7. Sprinkle shredded cheese and sauce over the baked meatballs.

8. Return the dish into the oven and bake until the shredded cheese melts for 10 minutes to 15 minutes.

Nutritional Information/serving

Calories 427 kcal, Fat 30g, Protein 33g, Carbohydrates 5g

Herbed Bacon with Green Beans

Preparation Time: 5 minutes

Cook Time: 10 minutes

Serve: 4 servings

Ingredients

1 tbsp ghee

Salt

1 (crushed) garlic clove

1/4 cup parsley (chopped)

1/4 cup basil (chopped)

3 strips (diced) bacon

3/4 lbs. (trimmed) green beans

Preparation

1. Add water and green beans into a pot, bring to a boil.

2. Transfer the boiled green beans into a steamer basket and steam for 4 minutes until it is soft.

3. In a pan, add in the diced bacon and fry until it is lightly crisped and golden.

4. Add in salt and crushed garlic clove into the pan, stir and cook until the garlic is lightly brown.

5. Turn off the heat and transfer the cooked garlic into a bowl.

6. Drain the water from the steamed beans and add the green beans into the garlic bowl.

7. In the garlic bowl, add in ghee, parsley and basil.

8. Stir until combined and serve.

Nutritional Information/serving

Calories 63 kcal, Protein 2g, Net Carbs 3.9g, Dietary Fiber 3.5g, Carbohydrates 7.4g, Fat 3.7g

Thai Red Beef Curry

Preparation Time: 15 minutes

Cook Time: 4 hours 10 minutes

Serve: 4 servings

Ingredients

3/4 teaspoon salt

1/2 fresh lime (juice & zest))

1 (14-oz) can coconut cream

1 tsp powdered turmeric

1/4 cup (warmed) bone broth, beef

2 tbsps (sugar free) Thai red curry paste

2-2 1/2 lbs. (cubed) chuck steak

Preparation

1. Heat up the oven to 210°F.

2. Add bone broth, salt, turmeric powder, lime zest, lime juice and Thai red curry paste into a big bowl.

3. Whisk until the bone broth mixture is combined.

4. Add in the coconut cream and the cubed chunk steak into the bone broth bowl. Stir until the steak is well coated.

5. In an oven safe pot, transfer the bone broth mixture and cover the pot with a lid.

6. Transfer the pot into the oven and bake steak for two hours.

7. Stir the steak in the pot and return the pot into the oven without covering with lid.

8. Bake the steak again for an additional hour to 1 1/2 hours or until the steak falls apart easily and soft.

9. Transfer the baked steak from the pot into a bowl and let stand to cool.

10. Return the oven safe pot into the oven with the steak juice and increase the oven heat to 320°F.

11. Cook the steak juice in the oven until the juice reduced by 1/2 in size for 40 minutes.

12. Take oven safe pot from the oven and add in the set aside baked steak back into the pot.

13. Serve red beef curry with steamed greens and zoodles if desired.

Nutritional Information/serving

Calories 656 kcal, Protein 82.7g, Net Carbs 1.2g, Dietary Fiber 0.1g, Carbohydrates 1.3g, Fat 32.9g

Shredded Mexican Beef

Preparation Time: 15 minutes

Cook Time: 7 hours

Serve: 8 servings

Ingredients

1 cup (roughly chopped) cilantro stems

1/2 cup water

2 tsps coriander, ground

2 tsps cumin, ground

1/2 tsp pepper

1 tsp salt

2 tsps turmeric, ground

3 1/2 lbs. beef shank

4 (crushed) garlic cloves

Preparation

1. Add cilantro stems, coriander, cumin, pepper, salt and turmeric into a small bowl. Mix until combined.

2. Coat each beef shank piece in the coriander mixture lightly and transfer into a slow cooker.

3. Gently add water, crushed garlic and chopped cilantro stems into the slow cooker.

4. Cook the beef shank until it is very tender for 6 hours to 7 hours on low.

5. Shred the cooked beef shank with two forks and serve.

Nutritional Information/serving

Calories 656 kcal, Fat 48.5g, Net Carbs 1g, Dietary Fiber 0.4g, Carbohydrates 1.4g, Protein 50.2g

Skirt Steak Pot Roast

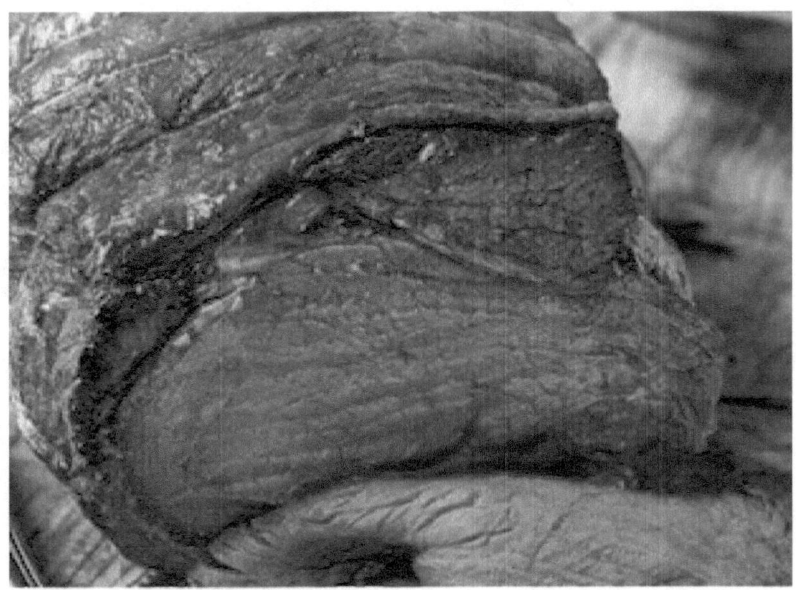

Preparation Time: 10 minutes

Cook Time: 8 hours

Serve: 2 servings

Ingredients

1.5 tbsps apple cider vinegar

3 tbsps butter (unsalted)

2 tbsps MCT oil

1 tsp oregano (dried)

1 tbsp turmeric (ground)

2 tbsps salt

1 lb. skirt steak

Preparation

1. In a bowl, add oregano, ground turmeric, salt and skirt steak. Toss to coat the steak.

2. In a slow cooker, transfer the coated steak, add in butter and MCT oil.

3. Cook steak for 6 hours to 8 hours on low.

4. Transfer the cooked steak into a bowl and use a fork to shred the steak.

5. Add apple cider vinegar into the shredded steak bowl, stir together and serve.

Nutritional Information/serving

Calories 734 kcal, Protein 46.4g, Dietary Fiber 1.0g, Carbohydrates 2.6g, Fat 59.8g

Swedish Parsley Meatballs

Preparation Time: 15 minutes

Cook Time: 35 minutes

Serve: 20 meatballs

Ingredients (meatball)

2 tbsps coconut oil

1 large egg

1/2 cup (minced) onion

1/2 tsp nutmeg

1/2 tsp allspice

1 tsp black pepper

1 tsp powdered garlic

1 tsp powdered onion

1 tsp parsley (dried)

1 tbsp coconut flour

2 tsps salt

2 lbs. beef, ground

Sauce

1 cup coconut cream.

Fish sauce (splash)

2 tbsps coconut aminos

2 thyme sprigs

2" piece lime peel

1 tbsp Dijon mustard

1 1/2 cups bone broth

1 tbsp gelatin

1 tbsp coconut flour

3 tbsps coconut oil

Preparation

1. On med-low heat, place a big pan of 16" over heat.

2. Add egg, onion, nutmeg, allspice, black pepper, garlic powder, onion powder, parsley, coconut flour, salt and ground beef into a big bowl.

3. Mix the ground beef mixture together and roll out 20 meatballs from the beef mixture.

4. Increase the heat to med heat and add the coconut oil into the pan.

5. In the pan with the coconut oil, add in the meatballs and cook until golden for 15 minutes.

6. Flip the meatballs at every 3 minutes interval during the cooking process.

7. On a plate, add the cooked meatballs and use a foil to cover the meatballs.

8. On med-heat, place another pan over heat and add in 3 tablespoons of coconut oil.

9. Add in coconut flour into the pan and stir together until it is lightly golden.

10. In a bowl, add the bone broth and gelatin.

11. Mix and pour the bone broth mixture into the pan, stir until combined.

12. Add thyme, lime, fish sauce, coconut aminos and Dijon mustard into the pan.

13. Bring mixture to simmer, for 15 minutes to 20 minutes.

14. Stir in the coconut cream into the pan and simmer until the mixture thickens.

15. Remove foil from the meatballs and transfer meatballs into the sauce in the pan.

16. Simmer and flip meatballs to coat with sauce for a few minutes and serve.

Nutritional Information/serving

Calories 467 kcal, Protein 32g, Dietary Fiber 2g, Carbohydrates 6g, Fat 32g

Creamy Pork Chops

Preparation Time: 10 minutes

Cook Time: 15 minutes

Serve: 4 servings

Ingredients

1/2 cup heavy cream

1 cup chicken broth

3 tbsps butter

Pepper

Salt

4 pork chops, boneless

Preparation

1. On med-heat, place a big pan over heat and add in the butter.

2. Heat the butter until melted and add in the boneless pork chops. Season pork chops with pepper and salt.

3. Cook until it is golden, and turn the pork chops.

4. Season the turned pork side with pepper and salt, cook again until it is golden.

5. Add in a cup of chicken broth and cook for 10 minutes until the broth is almost evaporated.

6. Transfer the cooked pork chops into a bowl and turn off the heat.

7. Add in 1/2 cup of heavy cream into the pan, frequently stir with a wooden spoon, for a few minutes until the cream thickens and is warm.

8. Serve pork chops with cream sauce.

Nutritional Information/serving

Calories 350 kcal, Protein 27.4g, Dietary Fiber 0.1g, carbohydrates 1.0g, Fat 26.6g

Keto Broccoli and Beef

Preparation Time: 15 minutes

Cook Time: 15 minutes

Serve: 4 servings

Ingredients

1/3 cup water

Cooked cauliflower rice (hot)

1/4 cup soy sauce

2 tsps garlic (minced)

1 lb. (slice into small florets) broccoli, fresh

1 lb. (slice into thin strips) top sirloin

1/4 tsp black pepper

2 tbsps cornstarch

3 tbsps vegetable oil

Preparation

1. On med-high heat, place a big pan over heat and add in two tbsps of vegetable oil.

2. In a medium bowl, add in black pepper and cornstarch. Stir until combined.

3. Add in sirloin strips into the cornstarch mixture and stir together until the strips are evenly coated.

4. Add the coated sirloin strips into the heated vegetable oil and stir-cook, for 4 minutes to 5 minutes, until the strips are lightly brown.

5. Transfer the cooked strips into a bowl and let stand.

6. Adjust heat to med-heat and add in a tbsp of vegetable oil into the pan.

7. Add in minced garlic and sliced broccoli into the pan. Stir-cook for 3 minutes to 4 minutes, until the broccoli is soft.

8. Add water, soy sauce and the reserved sirloin strips into the pan.

9. Stir-cook for 3 minutes to 4 minutes, until the sauce thickens.

10. Serve the beef sauce over cooked cauliflower rice.

Nutritional Information/serving

Calories 415 kcal, Protein 46.0g, Dietary Fiber 9.2g, Carbohydrates 24.2g, Fat 16.7g

Yummy Swiss Tender Steak

Preparation Time: 10 minutes

Cook Time: 9 hours

Serve: 3 servings

Ingredients

1 tsp smoked paprika

1/2 tsp powdered garlic

1 tsp pepper

1/2 tsp salt

2 tsps Oregano

1 (sliced) onion

14 oz tomato sauce

14 oz (diced & crushed) tomatoes stewed, canned

1 lb. steak, cubed

Preparation

1. In a 5-quart slow cooker, add the steak and sliced onions.

2. Add smoked paprika, garlic powder, pepper, salt, oregano, tomato sauce and tomatoes into a big bowl.

3. Stir the tomatoes mixture together and pour it over the steak in the slow cooker.

4. Cover the slow cooker with a lid.

5. Cook steak on high for 4 hours to 5 hours or 7 hours to 9 hours on low.

6. Serve the swiss tender steak with keto noodles.

Nutritional Information/serving

Calories 414 kcal, Protein 47.1g, Dietary Fiber 4.4g, Carbohydrates 16.5g, Fat 14.8g

Lime Greek Chicken

Preparation Time: 15 minutes

Cook Time: 1 hour 30 minutes

Serve: 4 servings

Ingredients

10 small (peeled and sliced) rutabaga

4 lbs. chicken drumsticks

1/3 cup olive oil

1/3 cup lime juice

1/2 tsp black pepper (ground)

2 tsps powdered garlic

1 tbsp oregano (dried)

2 tbsps kosher salt

Preparation

1. Add black pepper, garlic powder, oregano and salt into a small bowl. Stir together until combined.

2. Wash the rutabaga and divide into 4 equal part.

3. In a baking dish of 13 by 9", add the divided rutabaga and chicken drumsticks.

4. Season the chicken and rutabaga with the garlic powder mixture.

5. Sprinkle olive oil and lime juice over the chicken mixture in the dish.

6. Cover the baking dish with foil.

7. Heat up the oven to 350°F and place the baking dish into the oven.

8. Bake the chicken mixture for 1 hour.

9. Take dish out of the oven, uncover and adjust the temperature of the oven to 400°F.

10. Return the dish into the oven and bake until the chicken is slightly golden for 30 minutes.

11. Take baking dish out of the oven and serve lime Greek chicken.

Nutritional Information/serving

Calories 693 kcal, Protein 81.8g, Carbohydrates 8.1g, Fat 36.6g

APPETIZERS

Pimento Cheese (Southern Keto)

Preparation Time: 15 minutes

Cook Time: 20 minutes

Serve: 1 serving

Ingredients

½ teaspoon celery salt

1 teaspoon cayenne pepper

1 teaspoon paprika (smoked)

1 teaspoon Dijon mustard

½ cup mayo

1 cup red peppers, roasted (cut up, removed seeds and membranes)

2 cups cheddar cheese (grated)

2 cups cheddar cheese, extra-sharp (grated)

Preparation

1. Use a parchment paper to line a baking pan and add the red peppers with the cut-side facing down.

2. Heat up the oven to 450°F and transfer the baking pan into the oven.

3. Bake the red peppers for 20 minutes, until just charred and wrinkly.

4. Set aside the baked red pepper to cool and peel the pepper's skins. Discard the pepper skins.

5. Dice pepper and transfer into a bowl. Let stand.

6. Add in cayenne pepper, paprika, Dijon mustard, mayo, cheddar cheese and extra-sharp cheddar cheese.

7. Mix the cheddar cheese mixture together and season with celery salt.

Nutritional Information/Serving

Calories 1,705 kcal, Protein 51.0g, Dietary Fiber 7.0g, Carbohydrates 29.2 g, Fat 151.8g

Yummy Garlic Pasta

Preparation Time: 30 minutes

Cook Time: 5 minutes

Serve: 4 servings

Ingredients (pasta dough)

4 slivered garlic cloves

2 tbsps olive oil

56g butter, unsalted

2-4 tsps water

1 (lightly beaten) egg

2 tsps apple cider vinegar

1/4 tsp kosher salt

2 tsps xanthan gum

24g coconut flour

96g almond flour

Preparation

1. In a food processor, add in salt, xanthan gum, coconut flour and almond flour.

2. Process the almond flour mixture until combined well.

3. Add in 2 tbsps of apple cider vinegar into the almond flour mixture, process until combines evenly.

4. Add in the lightly beaten egg into the food processor.

5. Add in water, a tsp per time and process until a firm ball is formed with the dough.

6. In a cling film, transfer the dough, wrap and knead for 2 minutes through the plastic.

7. Transfer the dough into a bowl and let stand for 30 minutes.

Note: You can store dough in a fridge for 5 days.

8. To make a farfalle shape, transfer the dough onto a parchment paper and roll out with a rolling pin until a very thin point is reached.

9. Coarsely cut the dough into several 1-by-2 in. rectangles. Transfer the pasta into a freezer for 15 minutes to chill.

10. On low-heat, place a pan over heat, add olive oil and unsalted butter into the pan.

11. Add garlic cloves into the pan and cook until just brown.

12. Remove the pasta from the freezer, transfer into the pan and baste.

13. Cook until the garlic pasta changes color. Serve with desired toppings.

Nutritional Information/serving

Calories 176 kcal, Protein 7g, Dietary Fiber 4g, Carbohydrates 8g, Fat 13g

BREAD RECIPES

Herb Garlic Focaccia

Preparation Time: 10 minutes

Cook Time: 25 minutes

Serve: 8 servings

Ingredients

Fresh basil

Italian seasoning

2 tablespoons olive Oil (to drizzle)

2 teaspoons olive oil

1 tablespoons lime juice

2 eggs

1/2 teaspoon baking powder

1/2 teaspoon baking soda

1 teaspoon salt, flaky (more for topping)

1 teaspoon powdered garlic

1/2 tsp xanthan gum

1/4 cup coconut flour

1 cup almond flour

Preparation

1. Use parchment to line a round pan of 8" and heat up the oven to 350°F.

2. In a bowl, add in baking powder, baking soda, salt, garlic powder, xanthan gum, coconut flour and almond flour.

3. Whisk the almond flour mixture together until a smooth texture is formed.

4. In another bowl, add in 2 teaspoons of olive oil, lime juice and egg.

5. Beat together until the egg mixture combines.

6. Stir in the egg mixture into the almond flour bowl. Mix together until dough forms.

7. Transfer dough into the lined round pan.

8. Dip a spatula into water and smooth the upper part of the dough with the wet spatula.

9. Cover the round pan and place into the oven to bake for 10 minutes.

10. Take pan out of the oven. Drizzle 2 tablespoons of olive oil over the dough.

11. Return the pan into the oven and bake without covering the pan, for an additional 10 minutes to 15 minutes.

12. Take pan out of the oven and top with basil, Italian seasoning and salt as desired.

13. Set aside to cool, slice and serve.

Nutritional Information/serving

Calories 166 kcal, Protein 7g, Dietary Fiber 4g, Net Carbs 3g, Carbohydrates 7g, Fat 13g

Keto Collagen Bread

Preparation Time: 15 minutes

Cook Time: 40 minutes

Serve: 12 slices

Ingredients

Ghee (to grease dish)

Himalayan salt (pinch)

1 tsp xanthan gum

1 tsp baking powder

1 tbsp liquid coconut oil, unflavored

5 (separate yolks and egg whites) eggs

6 tbsps almond flour

1/2 cup collagen protein, unflavored

Preparation

1. Heat up the oven to 325°F.

2. Add ghee to the base of a ceramic loaf dish (1.5 quart) and grease the base only.

3. Add egg white into a big bowl and beat until stiff peaks are reached. Let stand.

4. Add salt, xanthan gum, baking powder, almond flour and collagen protein into a small bowl. Whisk together and let stand.

5. Add coconut oil and egg yolks into another small bowl, whisk together and let stand.

6. In the egg white bowl, add the collagen protein mixture and stir together until combined.

Note: The batter will be thick in texture.

7. Transfer the batter into the greased ceramic loaf dish and place into the preheated oven.

8. Bake the batter for 40 minutes, take dish out of the oven and set aside for an hour to 2 hours to cool.

9. Insert a knife around the ends of the dish to gently remove the bread.

10. Slice keto collagen bread and serve.

11. Store the remaining bread slices in a loosely covered container and preserve for 5 days in a refrigerator.

Nutritional Information/serving

Calories 77 kcal, Fat 5g, Net Carbs 0g, Dietary Fiber 1g, Carbohydrates 1g, Protein 7g

Keto Almond Flour Loaf

Preparation Time: 10 minutes

Cook Time: 35 minutes

Serve: 8 servings

Ingredients

1/2 teaspoon pink Himalayan salt

2 teaspoons baking powder

1/4 cup heavy cream

1/4 cup (melted) butter

1/4 cup monk fruit sweetener

2 large eggs

1 cup almond flour

Preparation

1. Heat up the oven to 350°F.

2. In a bowl, add in salt, baking powder, sweetener and almond flour. Mix together.

3. In another bowl, add in heavy cream, butter and eggs.

4. Mix until combined and stir in the egg mixture into the almond flour bowl. stir together.

5. In a 10 inches heavy bottom skillet, transfer the almond flour mixture and place into the preheated oven.

6. Bake until the upper part of the cornbread is golden for 30 minutes to 35 minutes.

7. Insert a fork in the middle of the cornbread and if the fork comes out clean, it means the cornbread is well cooked.

8. Set aside the almond flour loaf to cool for 5 minutes and serve.

Nutritional Information/Serving

Calories 115 kcal, Protein 2.3g, Carbohydrates 3.0g, Fat 11.8g, Dietary Fiber 0.4g

DESSERTS & SNACKS

Vanilla Cinnamon Rolls

Preparation Time: 15 minutes

Cook Time: 25 minutes

Serve: 10 servings

Ingredients (cinnamon roll)

Keto caramel sauce (chilled), to taste

1 tbsp apple cider vinegar

1 1/2 tsps baking powder

3 tsps Ceylon cinnamon

Salt (pinch)

4 eggs

2 tsps vanilla extract

3 tbsps birch xylitol

2 tbsps ghee

8 tbsps coconut flour

2 tbsps psyllium husks (ground)

2 cups macadamia nuts

Glaze

2 tsps erythritol

2 tbsps (melted) ghee

4 tbsps coconut cream

Preparation

1. Add macadamia nuts into a blender and blend until a fine consistency is reached. Set aside.

2. In a bowl, add in apple cider vinegar, baking powder, Ceylon cinnamon, salt, eggs, vanilla extract, birch xylitol, ghee, coconut flour and psyllium husks.

3. Transfer the coconut flour mixture into a fridge for 1 an hour to chill.

4. Use a parchment paper to line a baking tray and heat up the oven to 350°F.

5. Transfer the blended macadamia nuts onto the prepared baking tray. Use hands to roll out the dough.

6. Use the back of a spoon to form a big rectangle with the rolled-out dough.

7. Add the caramel sauce over the dough in the baking tray and spread the sauce close to the ends.

8. Gently roll the dough with sauce into a log shape and seal the rolled ends.

9. Slice the rolled dough into 10 rolls with a warm sharp knife.

10. Transfer the baking tray into the oven and bake for 25 minutes to 30 minutes.

11. In a blender, add erythritol, ghee and coconut cream. Blend until the mixture combines.

12. Transfer the vanilla cinnamon rolls onto plates, set aside to cool and dribble glaze over the roll.

Nutritional Information/serving

Calories 477 kcal, Protein 5.6g, Net Carbs 5g, Dietary Fiber 7.1g, Carbohydrates 17.1g, Fat 45.6g

Mouthwatering Keto Shepherd's Pie

Preparation Time: 20 minutes

Cook Time: 43 minutes

Serve: 6 servings

Ingredients

1 teaspoon thyme (dried)

1/4 cup parmesan cheese (grated)

1 cup cheese, shredded

1 cup heavy cream

2 (12 ounces) packages (cooked & drained) cauliflower rice

1 cup (chopped) tomatoes

1/2 cup (chopped) celery

3 (minced) garlic cloves

1/4 cup (chopped) yellow onion

1 pound beef, ground

1/4 cup olive oil

Preparation

1. Place a big pan over heat and add in olive oil.

2. Add in chopped celery, minced garlic, chopped yellow onions and ground beef into the warmed olive oil.

3. Cook the ground beef mixture until the beef is completely golden.

4. Put off the heat and add chopped tomatoes into the pan immediately.

5. In a casserole dish of 7 by 10", transfer the ground beef mixture.

6. Add dried thyme, parmesan cheese, shredded cheese, heavy cream and cauliflower rice into a food processor.

7. Process the cauliflower mixture until a mashed potato texture is reached.

8. Add cauliflower rice mixture over the ground beef mixture and spread.

9. Heat up the oven to 350°F.

10. Transfer the casserole dish into the oven and bake for 35 minutes to 40 minutes.

11. Set aside the shepherd's pie until lightly cool. Slice and serve the pie.

Nutritional Information/serving

Calories 302 kcal, Protein 14.0g, Fat 26.9g, Dietary Fiber 1.2g, Carbohydrates 4.3g

Chocolate Keto Cookies
Preparation Time: 10 minutes

Cook Time: 12 minutes

Serve: 15 servings

Ingredients

1/2 tsp xanthan gum

¼ tsp salt

½ tsp baking powder

1 tsp vanilla

1 egg

1 cup chocolate chips (no sugar)

½ cup butter

½ cup coconut sugar

1.5 cups almond flour

Preparation

1. Use parchment paper to line a baking tray and heat up the oven to 350°F.

2. In a bowl, add coconut sugar and butter.

3. Mix the butter mixture together with a hand mixer for 5 minutes on low.

4. Add in the vanilla, egg and almond flour (1/2 cup at a time) into the butter mixture.

5. Mix with hand mixer until the butter mixture is combined.

6. Add in xanthan gum, salt and baking powder into the butter mixture and mix for a minute more.

7. Add in the chocolate chips into the butter mixture. Mix the dough lightly.

8. Split dough into 15 equal cookies using a cookie scoop and transfer onto the prepared baking tray.

9. Flatten each cookie with a spoon and transfer the baking tray into the oven.

10. Bake the dough for 10 minutes to 12 minutes. Set aside the cookies to cool and crisp for few minutes.

11. Store the chocolate keto cookies in an airtight container.

12. Place the container in a refrigerator and store for 10 days.

Nutritional Information/serving

Calories 94 kcal, Protein 1.5g, Dietary Fiber 0.4g, Carbohydrates 3.7g, Fat 6.8g

Chilled Keto Fudge Pops

Preparation Time: 10 minutes

Cook Time: 10 minutes

Serve: 4 servings

Ingredients (cookies)

Liquid stevia

2 tablespoons collagelatin

2 egg yolks

1 tablespoon cacao butter

270 m coconut cream

1 teaspoon vanilla powder

2 tablespoons Brain Octane oil

Salt (a pinch)

1/2-1 tablespoon powdered chocolate, unsweetened

Preparation

1. Add all the ingredients into a small saucepan except egg yolks and stevia.

2. On low heat, place the saucepan with the chocolate powder mixture over heat.

3. Bring the chocolate powder mixture to simmer until the ingredients are combined and melted.

4. Take saucepan off heat and set aside to cool.

5. In an electric blender, add liquid stevia (as desired) and egg yolks.

6. Blitz egg yolks mixture until creamy and a fine texture form.

7. In an ice-block mold, transfer the creamy egg yolk mixture and place into a freezer until set.

8. Under warm water, run the molds until fudge pop comes off easily, for 1 minute to 2 minutes and serve.

Nutritional Information/serving

Calories 303 kcal, Protein 11g, Dietary Fiber 1g, Carbohydrates 6g, Fat 26g

Cacao Almond Oreos

Preparation Time: 15 minutes

Cook Time: 15 minutes

Serve: 10 servings

Ingredients (cookies)

Salt (a pinch)

1 egg

4 tbsps birch xylitol

1 tsp vanilla extract

3 tbsps coconut oil

1 tsp apple cider vinegar

1/2 tsp baking soda

1 1/2 cups almond meal (blanched)

1/4 cup powdered cacao

Filling

1 tsp vanilla extract

2 tbsps birch xylitol

3 tbsps coconut oil (melted)

3 tbsps cacao butter

1/2 cup cashews (pre-soaked)

Preparation

1. Use a silicone liner to line a baking pan and heat up the oven to 350°F.

2. In a bowl, add salt, egg, birch xylitol, vanilla extract, coconut oil, apple cider vinegar, baking soda, almond meal and cacao powder.

3. Stir the almond meal mixture together to form a dough; taste and add more salt if needed.

4. Place the dough on a parchment paper and use a rolling pin to roll out the cookie dough into a flat sheet.

5. Cut the dough into 20 even circles with a small cup.

6. On the lined baking pan, transfer the 20 dough circles and place into the oven for 15 minutes to bake. Set aside to cool.

7. In a blender, add vanilla extract, birch xylitol, coconut oil, cacao butter and cashews.

8. Blend the filling mixture until a fine texture is reached.

9. In the middle of each cookie, add a tsp of the filling, spread out with a spoon towards the ends and place another cookie over the spread cookie.

10. Repeat the above assembling-process with the remaining cookies, transfer into an airtight container and place into a fridge until it is set.

Nutritional Information/serving

Calories 269 kcal, Protein 6g, Net Carbs 2.6g, Dietary Fiber 3.2g, Carbohydrates 13g, Fat 25g

Brussels Sprouts Bake

Preparation Time: 5 minutes

Cook Time: 45 minutes

Serve: 2 servings

Ingredients

2 tsps turmeric (ground)

2 tsps salt

2 tbsps ghee

1 lb. (halved) Brussels sprouts

Preparation

1. Grease a baking sheet with 2 tablespoons of ghee and heat up the oven to 300°F.

2. Add the Brussels sprouts onto the greased baking sheet.

3. Season the Brussels sprouts with ground turmeric and sea salt.

4. Transfer the baking sheet into the oven and bake for 30 minutes to 45 minutes

5. Serve the baked Brussels Sprouts.

Nutritional Information/serving

Calories 240 kcal, Protein 8.0g, Dietary Fiber 9.0g, Carbohydrates 22.1g, Fat 15.1g

Cheesy Almond Biscuits

Preparation Time: 5 minutes

Cook Time: 13 minutes

Serve: 12 servings

Ingredients

1/2 Cup cheese, shredded

4 tbsps (melted) butter

1/2 cup sour cream

2 eggs

1/2 tsp powdered onion

1/2 tsp powdered garlic

1 tbsp baking powder

1/4 tsp salt

1 1/2 Cups almond flour

Preparation

1. Heat up the oven to 450°F.

2. In a bowl, add onion powder, garlic powder, baking powder, salt and almond flour. Mix until combined.

3. In another bowl, add in shredded cheese, butter, sour cream and eggs. Mix until it is well combined.

4. Grease a muffin tin and use a spoon to drop a dollop of the batter into the muffin cavities.

5. Transfer the muffin tin into the preheated oven and bake for 10 minutes to 13 minutes.

Nutritional Information/serving

Calories 164 kcal, Dietary Fiber 1.6g, Fat 14.6g, Protein 5.9g, Carbohydrates 4.6g

Chocolate Lava Cake

Preparation Time: 10 minutes

Cook Time: 10 minutes

Serve: 2 servings

Ingredients (cake)

1/8 cup chunks chocolate

1/8 tsp sea salt

1 tbsp erythritol, granulated

2 tbsps erythritol, powdered

1 tsp vanilla extract

2 (room temperature & beaten) eggs

2 oz ghee

1 tbsp almond flour

2 oz (85% cocoa) high-quality chocolate

Garnish

Coconut milk (powdered)

Fresh raspberries

Almond butter

Sea salt flakes

Preparation

1. Use ghee to grease 2 ramekins and heat up the oven to 350°F.

2. On low heat, place a small saucepan over heat and add in 2 oz of ghee and chocolate until melted.

3. Stir the chocolate until combined and let stand.

4. Add salt, vanilla extract and eggs into a bowl and whisk with a hand mixer until it is frothy.

5. In the saucepan with the chocolate, add almond flour, erythritol and the whisked egg mixture.

6. Stir the egg mixture together until combined.

7. Divide batter in two. Share one half of the batter between the greased ramekins, and add in 1/8 cup of chocolate chunks. Add the remaining batter over the chocolate chunks in the ramekins.

8. Transfer the ramekins into the preheated oven and bake until the top is set for 9 minutes.

9. Set aside the chocolate lava cake to cool.

10. Transfer onto plates and garnish with coconut milk, raspberries, almond flour and sea salt flakes.

Nutritional Information/serving

Calories 559 kcal, Protein 9.7g, Net Carbs 4.4g, Dietary Fiber 5.5g, Carbohydrates 27.9g, Fat 52g

Cookie Ice Cream Sandwich

Preparation Time: 15 minutes

Cook Time: 15 minutes

Serve: 4 servings

Ingredients (cookie)

1/3 cup chopped chocolate (sugar free)

Salt (a pinch)

1 tsp apple cider vinegar

1/2 tsp baking powder

1 egg

2 tsps vanilla extract

Birch xylitol

3 tbsps collagen protein

3 tbsps (melted) ghee

2 cups almond flour, blanched

Ice cream

2 tsps vanilla extract

1/4–1/3 cup powdered cocoa

1/4 scant cup water (filtered)

3.5 tbsps sweetener (granulated)

3 tbsps (melted) coconut oil (additional 2 tsp coconut oil)

Scant 1 tsp XCT Oil

6 tbsps XCT oil

3.5 tbsps (melted) cacao butter

7 tbsps (melted) ghee

1 tsp apple cider vinegar

4 egg yolks

4 eggs

Preparation

1. Grease 2 baking trays and line the trays with parchment paper. Heat up oven to 340°F.

2. In a bowl, add baking powder, salt, collagen protein and blanched almond flour.

3. Add in the chocolate, egg, vanilla extract, birch xylitol, ghee and apple cider vinegar. Stir until combined.

Note: Taste dough and add more birch xylitol as desired.

4. On a work surface, add the dough and roll into balls.

5. Transfer the dough balls to the prepared baking trays.

6. Press down each dough ball and shape with hands.

7. Transfer the baking trays into the oven and bake until it is brown for 15 minutes.

8. Set aside the cookies for 5 minutes to cool before transferring cookies onto a wire rack.

9. In an electric blender, add granulated sweetener, vanilla extract, cocoa powder, water, coconut oil, XCT oil, cacao butter, ghee, apple cider vinegar, egg yolks and yolk.

10. Blitz the ice cream ingredients together for a minute to 2 minutes.

Note: Taste the blitz ice cream mixture and add more sweetener as desired.

11. In an ice cream maker, pour the ice cream mixture and churn it for 15 minutes to 20 minutes.

12. In a container, add in the ice cream and transfer into a freezer, for 10 minutes to 15 minutes to set.

13. On a cookie, scoop a spoonful of the ice cream over a cookie.

14. Place another cookie over the ice cream and lightly press down the cookies until sticks together.

14. Make four ice cream sandwiches with the remaining cookies by repeating the process above.

Nutritional Information/serving

Calories 662 kcal, Protein 25g, Net Carbs 6.8g, Dietary Fiber 4g, Carbohydrates 15g, Fat 51g

Cinnamon Chocolate Doughnuts

Preparation Time: 5 minutes

Cook Time: 8 minutes

Serve: 5 servings

Ingredients (donuts)

Coconut oil

1 tbsp butter (softened)

1 tsp vanilla bean (powdered)

3 tsps Ceylon cinnamon

1 tbsp (sifted) powdered cacao

Salt (a pinch)

1 tsp apple cider vinegar

1 tsp baking powder

2-3 tbsps sweetener, granulated

2 eggs

3-4 tbsps coconut milk

1/2 cup (sifted) green banana flour

Garnish

Cacao nibs

Coconut (shredded)

Preparation

1. Use coconut oil to grease a doughnut tray and heat up the oven to 350°F.

2. In a bowl, add butter, vanilla bean, Ceylon cinnamon, cacao powder, salt, apple cider vinegar, baking powder, sweetener, eggs, coconut milk and green banana flour.

3. Stir the green banana flour mixture until combined evenly.

4. Fill 3/4 of the greased doughnut molds with the banana flour mixture and transfer the doughnut tray into the preheated oven.

5. Bake batter until the doughnuts are well cooked for 8 minutes.

6. Take the doughnut tray out of the oven and gently transfer each doughnut onto a wire rack to cool.

7. Serve the cinnamon chocolate doughnuts, garnish with cacao nibs and shredded coconut.

Nutritional Information/serving

Calories 112 kcal, Protein 3g, Net Carbs 6.4g, Dietary Fiber 2.4g, Fat 6.6g, Carbohydrates 8.8g

Keto Pecan Pie

Preparation Time: 25 minutes

Cook Time: 1 hour 2 minutes

Serve: 10 servings

Ingredients (crust)

1/2 teaspoon pink Himalayan salt

3/4 teaspoon vanilla extract

3/4 tablespoon coconut oil

6 tablespoons butter

3 tablespoons erythritol

1.5 large eggs

3/4 cup coconut flour

Filling

1 1/2 cups (coarsely chopped) raw Pecans

1 teaspoon vanilla extract

10 tablespoon maple syrup (sugar free)

2 tablespoons butter

10 tablespoons erythritol

2 large eggs

Preparation

1. In a bowl, add salt, erythritol and coconut flour. Mix together and let stand.

2. In another bowl, add 3/4 teaspoon of vanilla extract, coconut oil, butter and eggs. Stir until combined.

3. Stir in the coconut flour mixture gently into the butter mixture. Mix together until combined.

Note: The coconut flour mixture will form tender dough.

4. Grease a pie pan of 8" and transfer the soft dough into the pie pan.

5. Gently press down the dough into the sides and base of the greased pie pan with hands.

6. Heat up an oven to 350°F.

7. Transfer the pie pan into the oven and bake for 12 minutes.

Note: Check the pie to prevent burning ends.

8. Remove the pie pan from the oven and leave the oven on. Set the crust aside to cool.

9. In a bowl, add vanilla extract, maple syrup, butter, erythritol and eggs.

10. Stir the maple syrup mixture until combined.

11. Add the coarsely chopped pecans over the baked crust in a layer. Add the maple syrup mixture over the pecans.

12. Cover the pie filling with the crust and transfer the pie into the preheated oven for 50 minutes to bake.

13. Remove the pie pan from the oven and set aside for a couple of hours to cool.

14. Slice the pecan pie and serve.

Nutritional Information/Serving

Calories 259.2 kcal, Protein 4.65g, Dietary Fiber 4.9g, Carbohydrates 9.3g, Fat 25g, Net carbs 4.4g

Scrumptious Butter Cake

Preparation Time: 10 minutes

Cook Time: 50 minutes

Serve: 16 servings

Ingredients

1 cup water

1/2 cup heavy whipping cream

3 teaspoons vanilla extract

7 large eggs

1 cup swerve

1 cup (softened & salted) butter

1/2 teaspoon Salt

1 teaspoon baking Powder

1/4 cup protein egg white

1 cup coconut flour

2.5 cups almond flour

Preparation

1. In a mixing bowl, add swerve and butter.

2. Use a mixer to mix until the swerve mixture is combined.

3. Add in water, heavy whipping cream, vanilla extract, eggs, salt, baking powder, egg white protein, coconut flour and almond flour into the swerve mixture bowl.

4. Stir the swerve mixture together until combined.

Note: The texture of the batter will be easy to spread and thick.

5. Use cooking spray to coat a bundt pan and sprinkle coconut flour into the pan.

6. Dust the pan to shake off the excess coconut flour in the pan completely.

7. Heat up an oven to 350°F.

8. Transfer the batter into the bundt pan and place pan into the preheated oven.

9. Bake cake is until browned, for 45 minutes to 50 minutes.

Note: Insert a toothpick into the cake. The cake is set when the toothpick comes out clean.

Nutritional Information/Serving

Calories 267 kcal, Dietary Fiber 1.9g, Fat 25g, Protein 8.2g, Carbohydrates 7.1g

SMOOTHIES & DRINKS

Mixed Berry Cheesecake Smoothie

Preparation Time: 5 minutes

Cook Time: 0 minutes

Serve: 1 serving

Ingredients

Himalayan salt (a pinch)

7-10 drops monk fruit extract

1/2 cup mixed berries (frozen)

1 teaspoon vanilla extract

1 ounce cream cheese

2 tablespoons avocado

1/2 cup almond milk, unsweetened

Preparation

1. In an electric blender, add salt, monk fruit extract, mixed berries, vanilla extract, cream cheese, avocado and almond milk.

2. Blend the cream cheese mixture on high speed until a fine texture is reached.

Note: To thin out the smoothie, add additional unsweetened almond milk as desired.

Nutritional Information/Serving

Calories 158 kcal, Dietary Fiber 6g, Fat 11g, Protein 3g, Carbohydrates 12g

Pecan Chocolate Shake

Preparation Time: 5 minutes

Cook Time: 0 minutes

Serve: 1 serving

Ingredients

3-4 ice cubes

2 1/2 teaspoons stevia

1/8 teaspoon Himalayan salt

2 tablespoons cocoa powder, unsweetened

2 tablespoons avocado

10 pecan halves, raw

1 1/3 cups almond milk, unsweetened

Preparation

1. In an electric blender, add ice cubes, stevia, Himalayan salt, cocoa powder, avocado, raw pecan halves and almond milk.

2. Blend the pecan mixture until a fine texture is reached.

3. Pour the pecan mixture into a glass and serve.

Nutritional Information/Serving

Calories 247 kcal, Dietary Fiber 8g, Fat 20g, Protein 5g, Carbohydrates 12g

Almond Protein Berry Smoothie

Preparation Time: 5 minutes

Cook Time: 0 minutes

Serve: 1 serving

Ingredients

1/3 cup strawberries (frozen)

1/3 cup water

1/2 cup almond milk

1/2 scoop (vanilla) protein powder

A tablespoon almond butter

Preparation

1. In an electric blender, add strawberries, water, almond milk, protein powder and almond butter.

2. Blend the mixture almond milk mixture until combined.

Note: Thin out with water if the smoothie is too thick.

Macadamia Cacao Creamie

Preparation Time: 5 minutes

Cook Time: 0 minutes

Serve: 1 1/2 cups

Ingredients

Collagen peptides (to taste)

1 tbsp cacao

2 tbsps chia seed

1 tbsp coconut butter

1 tsp MCT oil

2 tbsps macadamia nuts

1 cup vanilla almond milk, unsweetened

Preparation

1. In an electric blender, add collagen peptides, cacao, chia seed, coconut butter, MCT oil, macadamia nuts and vanilla almond milk.

2. Blend the vanilla almond milk mixture on high speed until a fine texture is reached.

Nutritional Information/Serving

Calories 460 kcal, Dietary Fiber 14g, Carbohydrates 22g, Protein 10g, Fat 41g

Keto Green Smoothie

Preparation Time: 5 minutes

Cook Time: 0 minutes

Serve: 1 1/2 cups

Ingredients

¼ tsp powdered turmeric

1 lemon (juice only)

2 tbsps hemp seeds

2 tbsps parsley

1–2 dandelion leaves

1 big handful leafy greens, dark

1/2 cucumber

1 tbsp MCT oil

1/2 avocado

1 cup water, filtered

Preparation

1. In an electric blender, add turmeric, lemon juice, hemp seeds, parsley, dandelion leaves, dark leafy greens, cucumber, MCT oil, avocado and water.

2. Blend the dark leafy greens mixture until a fine texture is formed.

Nutritional Information/Serving

Calories 360 kcal, Dietary Fiber 8g, Carbohydrates 12g, Protein 10g, Fat 33g

Vanilla Spinach Protein Smoothie

Preparation Time: 5 minutes

Cook Time: 0 minutes

Serve: 1 serving

Ingredients

Ice cubes (a handful)

Stevia

1 teaspoon vanilla extract

Spinach (a handful)

1 tablespoon sunflower seed butter

½ avocado

Collagen protein powder (a scoop)

1/2 tablespoon MCT oil

½ cup coconut milk

Preparation

1. In a high-speed blender, add ice cubes, stevia, sunflower seed butter, avocado, collagen protein powder, MCT oil and coconut milk.

2. Blend the coconut milk mixture until a smooth texture is reached and serve.

Nutritional Information/Serving

Calories 510 kcal, Carbohydrates 22g, Protein 18g, Fat 51.64g

SOUP RECIPES

Keto Gumbo

Preparation Time: 15 minutes

Cook Time: 30 minutes

Serve: 7 servings

Ingredients

6 cups chicken broth

2 large bay leaves

1 teaspoon xanthan gum

1 tablespoons creole seasoning

1 pound shrimp

1 (11 ounces) sliced at an angle, andouille sausage, smoked

1 cup green bell peppers (chopped)

1 cup celery (chopped)

1/2 cup yellow onions, raw (chopped)

1/2 cup olive oil

Preparation

1. Add olive oil (one tablespoon) into a medium pot.

2. Add chopped bell peppers, celery and onions into the pot.

3. Cook the bell pepper mixture until the onions becomes translucent.

4. Add in shrimp and smoked andouille sausage into the bell pepper mixture. Cook for an additional 2 minutes.

5. Add creole seasoning, remaining olive oil, chicken broth, bay leaves and xanthan gum into the pot.

6. Stir bell pepper mixture together, bring to just a boil and simmer on low heat.

7. Cook until the chicken broth is reduced in size, for 10 minutes to 15 minutes.

8. Set aside the keto gumbo to cool and serve.

Nutritional Information/serving

Calories 252 kcal, Protein 18g, Dietary Fiber 2g, Carbohydrates 6g, Fat 18g

Celery Chicken Soup

Preparation Time: 10 minutes

Cook Time: 2 hour 10 minutes

Serve: 14 (1 cup) servings

Ingredients

Liquid stevia

1 spaghetti squash, medium

Black pepper

Salt

1 medium (whole) bay leaf

1 tablespoon Italian seasoning

10 cups chicken broth

1 cup (diced) onion

1 cup (diced) celery

1 cup (diced) carrots

2 cups (cooked & shredded) chicken

Preparation

1. Add stevia, pepper, salt, bay leaf, Italian seasoning, chicken broth, onion, celery, carrots and chicken into a big pot.

2. Place the pot over heat and bring the chicken mixture to boiling.

3. Adjust the heat to low heat, simmer the chicken mixture for an hour and set aside.

4. On a baking pan, add the spaghetti squash and use a knife to poke holes in the squash.

5. Heat up the oven to 375°F and place the baking pan into the oven.

6. Bake the spaghetti squash until a fork pierces through easily, for 40 minutes to 60 minutes.

7. Set aside spaghetti squash to cool, cut into half and scoop out the strands with a fork.

8. Remove bay leaf from the soup and add in the spaghetti squash.

9. Stir and serve celery chicken soup.

Nutritional Information/serving

Calories 44 kcal, Dietary Fiber 1g, Carbohydrates 4g, Protein 5g, Fat 1g

Slow Cooked Cauliflower Soup

Preparation Time: 25 minutes

Cook Time: 6 hours 35 minutes

Serve: 10 servings

Ingredients

3 cloves garlic

1 tsp (chopped) Onion

6 oz cream cheese

½ butter stick

1 cup heavy cream

2.5 cups cheddar cheese

4 cups broth (chicken)

10 bacon slices

2 large cauliflower, head (cut into florets)

Other Ingredients

2 tsps thyme

2 tsps Kosher salt

¼ tsp red pepper (crushed)

5 (chopped) cloves garlic

¼ cup olive oil

Preparation

1. Use foil to line a baking sheet.

2. In a bowl, add cauliflower florets, thyme, red pepper, salt, garlic and olive oil.

3. Toss to coat the cauliflower florets and transfer onto the prepared baking sheet.

4. Heat up the oven to 400°F, place the baking sheet into the oven and bake for 25 minutes to 30 minutes.

5. In a pan, add bacon slices.

6. Place the pan over heat and cook the bacon.

7. Transfer the cooked bacon into a bowl and set aside.

8. Add garlic and onion into the bacon fat and cook for 2 minutes to 3 minutes.

8. Add every ingredient into the slow cooker, excluding the heavy cream, cheddar cheese and cream cheese, and cook for 4 hours to 6 hours.

9. Puree the cauliflower soup until a creamy and smooth consistency is reached, using a handheld blender.

10. Add in 2 cups of cheddar cheese, cream cheese and heavy cream into the blender and puree.

11. Serve cauliflower soup and top with scallions, cooked bacon, cheddar cheese, cream cheese and heavy cream.

Nutritional Information/serving

Calories 446 kcal, Protein 14.3g, Dietary Fiber 2.5g, Carbohydrates 9.1g, Fat 40.4g

Creamy Turkey Taco Soup

Preparation Time: 10 minutes

Cook Time: 15 minutes

Serve: 10 servings

Ingredients

2–3 tbsps taco seasoning

4 Ounces green chiles

2 (14 Ounces) can diced tomatoes with juices

4 cups bone broth

4 (minced) cloves garlic

1 (8 Ounces) cream cheese block

1/2 Small (diced) Onion

1 lb. turkey, ground

Preparation

1. On med-high heat, place a skillet over heat.

2. Add in the diced onions and ground turkey. Cook until the ground turkey is golden.

3. Add taco seasoning, green chiles and garlic. Stir and cook for a minute to 2 minutes.

4. Add in the diced tomatoes with juice and bone broth into the ground turkey mixture.

5. Simmer the ground turkey mixture on low heat for 5 minutes.

6. Add in the cream cheese block, stir together and cook for about 5 minutes.

7. Serve creamy turkey taco soup and garnish as desired.

Nutritional Information/serving

Calories 107 kcal, Protein 12.3g, Dietary Fiber 1g, Carbohydrates 4.5g, Fat 4.6g

Bacon Cheeseburger Soup

Preparation Time: 15 minutes

Cook Time: 6 hours 10 minutes

Serve: 8 servings

Ingredients

1/2 cup heavy cream

4 Oz cream cheese

1/2 cup cheddar cheese (shredded)

1 tsp black pepper

Sea salt (a pinch)

4 (minced) garlic cloves

1/2 tsp powdered chili

2.5 tbsps tomato paste

1/2 cup onion (chopped)

4 cups beef broth

8 bacon slices

1.5 lbs. beef, ground

Toppings

Dill pickles (sliced)

Sour cream

1/2 cup cheddar cheese (shredded)

Preparation

1. Place a skillet over heat and add in the bacon slices.

2. Cook the bacon slices and transfer into a bowl.

3. Crumble the cooked bacon slices and let stand.

4. Add in the chili powder, chopped onions, minced garlic and ground beef into the skillet.

5. Stir the ground beef mixture together and cook until the ground beef is brown.

6. In a slow cooker, add in the black pepper, salt, tomato paste, beef broth and the cooked ground beef mixture.

7. Stir together and cook the soup for 5 hours on low.

8. Add in heavy cream, 1/2 cup of cream cheese and shredded cheddar cheese into the slow cooker.

9. Stir together and cook the soup for an additional 1 hour.

10. Serve bacon cheeseburger soup and top with dill pickles, sour cream, shredded cheddar cheese and crumbled bacon.

Nutritional Information/serving

Calories 335 kcal, Protein 27.2g, Dietary Fiber 0.3g, Carbohydrates 3.4g, Fat 23.3g

Chicken Noodle Soup

Preparation Time: 10 minutes

Cook Time: 60 minutes

Serve: 4 servings

Ingredients

2 cups daikon noodles (spiralized)

1/3 tsp fresh pepper (ground)

1 tsp salt

½ tsp oregano (dried)

½ tsp basil (dried)

6 cups chicken stock

¾ cup green onion (chopped only the green part)

1 cup carrots (diced)

1 cup radish (diced)

1 lb. chicken thighs, boneless and skinless

2 tbsps coconut oil

Preparation

1. In a big saucepan, add in the chicken thighs and coconut oil.

2. On med heat, place the saucepan over heat and cook the chicken thighs until it starts to cook though, for 15 minutes.

3. Use a fork to shred the chicken thighs and add chopped green onions, carrots and radish into the saucepan.

4. Cook chicken thighs mixture for an additional 15 minutes.

5. Stir the chicken thighs mixture together and add in fresh pepper, salt, oregano and basil into the saucepan.

6. Place a lid over the saucepan and cook until the soup boils.

7. Bring the mixture to simmer for 25 minutes.

8. Serve soup with the daikon noodles.

Nutritional Information/serving

Calories 267 kcal, Protein 21.2g, Dietary Fiber 4.7g, Carbohydrates 8.6g, Fat 15.8g

Cauliflower Rice Soup with Chicken

Preparation Time: 5 minutes

Cook Time: 30 minutes

Serve: 6 servings

Ingredients

1/4 cup fresh parsley, flat leaf

2 cups coconut milk

2 cups cauliflower rice

1 chicken breast, boneless skinless

1 bay Leaf

4 cups chicken broth

1 tsp thyme, fresh

Pepper

Salt

2 stalks (diced) celery

2 (peeled & diced) carrots

1 (chopped) small Onion

2 tbsps olive oil

Preparation

1. Place a big pot over heat and add in 2 tablespoons of olive oil.

2. Add in the diced celery, carrots and chopped onion into the pot with the heated olive oil.

3. Cook the carrots mixture until the veggies starts to tenderize, for 5 minutes to 8 minutes.

4. Sprinkle the carrots mixture with thyme, pepper and salt to season. Stir together.

5. Add in the bay leaf and chicken broth into the carrot mixture and boil. Stir and simmer on low heat.

6. Add in the boneless skinless chicken breast into the pot, place a lid over the pot and simmer until the chicken breast is well cooked.

7. Transfer the cooked chicken breast into a bowl and shred with forks.

8. Remove the bay leaf from the soup and discard.

9. Add cauliflower rice and shredded chicken into the pot.

10. Stir chicken mixture together and simmer until the cauliflower is well cooked, for 5 minutes.

11. Add in the fresh parsley and coconut milk into the chicken mixture and cook until it is completely warm.

12. Sprinkle pepper and salt into the soup as desired. Stir and serve.

Nutritional Information/serving

Calories 340 kcal, Protein 9.7g, Dietary Fiber 15.9g, Carbohydrates 54.0g, Fat 7.8g

SIDE DISHES

Bacon Fried Cabbage

Preparation Time: 10 minutes

Cook Time: 46 minutes

Serve: 8 servings

Ingredients

1/4 teaspoon black pepper

1/2 teaspoon paprika

1 1/2 teaspoons sea salt

1 cabbage head, large (shredded)

4 cloves (minced) garlic

1 large (sliced into thick half-moons) sweet onion

8 bacon, slices

Preparation

1. In a big skillet, add the sliced bacon and arrange in a layer.

2. At med-heat, place the skillet over heat, cook bacon slices for 5 minutes, turn and cook the other side until it is golden for another 5 minutes.

3. Take bacon slices from the skillet, set aside and leave the fat in the skillet.

4. Add in the sliced sweet onion into the fat in the skillet and cook until the onion is golden for 10 minutes.

Note: Don't place a lid over the skillet while cooking the onion.

5. Use a spatula to create a space in the middle of the skillet, add in garlic and cook until it is aromatic for 1 minute.

6. Stir the cooked garlic with the onion together.

7. Add in pepper, paprika, salt and shredded cabbage into the skillet.

8. Place a lid over skillet and cook until the cabbage is soft for 15 minutes to 25 minutes.

Note: You can cook the cabbage in batches.

9. Chop the cooked bacon slices and transfer the bacon into the skillet with the cabbage.

10. Stir together and serve bacon fried cabbage.

Nutritional Information/Serving

Calories 143 kcal, Dietary Fiber 4g, Net Carbs 8g, Carbohydrates 12g, Protein 5g, Fat 9g

Keto Herbed Cornbread

Preparation Time: 5 minutes

Cook Time: 35 minutes

Serve: 6 servings

Ingredients

Cooking spray

2 cups chicken broth

2 oz celery (finely diced)

3 oz onion (finely diced)

4 tbsps melted butter

3 eggs

1/2 tsp salt

2 tsps baking powder

2 tbsps sage, ground

2 1/2 cups almond flour

Preparation

1. Use cooking spray to coat a baking dish of 13 by 9" and heat up the oven to 350°F.

2. Add salt, baking powder, ground sage and almond flour into a big bowl.

3. Whisk together until a smooth texture is formed.

4. Add in melted butter and eggs into the almond flour mixture. Whisk together until combined.

5. Gently add in the chicken broth, diced celery and onions into the almond flour bowl. Whisk together until combined.

Note: The texture of the dough will be runny and very thin.

6. In the sprayed baking dish, transfer dough and place into the oven.

7. Bake the cornbread until the middle is no longer jiggly and cornbread becomes golden at the top, for 35 minutes.

8. Set aside the herbed cornbread for 5 minutes to cool and serve.

Nutritional Information/serving

Calories 415 kcal, Protein 13.6g, Dietary Fiber 5.7g, Net Carbs 5.2g, Carbohydrates 10.9g, Fat 35g

Keto Green Beans

Preparation Time: 5 minutes

Cook Time: 50 minutes

Serve: 14 servings

Ingredients

Salt

1/4 teaspoon (minced) dried onion

1/2 teaspoon pepper

1/2 teaspoon salt garlic

1 tbsp Italian dressing

1 tbsp butter

2 tbsps bacon grease

4 cans (14.5 ounces) cut green beans

Preparation

1. On med-high heat, place a saucepan over heat.

2. In the saucepan, add in dried onion, pepper, garlic salt, Italian dressing, butter, bacon grease and green beans.

3. Place a lid over the saucepan and bring the green beans mixture to boiling, for 35 minutes to 45 minutes over med-heat.

4. Remove the lid and cook until the juice almost evaporates.

5. Sprinkle salt over the cooked green beans to taste.

Nutritional Information/serving

Calories 42 kcal, Protein 0.6g, Dietary Fiber 0.9g, Carbohydrates 2.6g, Fat 3.4g

Creamy Cauliflower Casserole

Preparation Time: 10 minutes

Cook Time: 15 minutes

Serve: 8 servings

Ingredients

Fresh chives

2 tbsps green onions

1/4 tsp black pepper

1/2 cup Jack cheese

1 1/2 cups cheddar cheese (shredded)

3 tbsps Butter

¼ cup heavy cream

1/2 cup sour cream

8 fried bacon strips

6 oz (cut into chunks) cream cheese

1 (chopped) cauliflower head

Salt

Preparation

1. Heat up the oven to 400°F.

2. In a pot, add water and bring to boiling.

3. Place a steamer basket on top of the pot and add in the chopped cauliflower to the basket.

4. Steam the cauliflower for 5 minutes until soft.

5. Get rid of the excess water.

6. In a bowl, transfer the steamed cauliflower and cover bowl.

7. Let the cauliflower sit for 2 minutes to 3 minutes.

8. Add in butter, heavy cream, sour cream, Jack cheese, a cup of shredded cheddar cheese and cream cheese into the cauliflower bowl.

9. Sprinkle black pepper and salt over the cauliflower mixture. Toss together until the mixture combines.

10. In an oven proof casserole dish, transfer the cauliflower mixture.

11. Sprinkle bacon and 1/2 cup of cheddar cheese over the cauliflower mixture.

12. Transfer the casserole dish into the oven, bake for 8 minutes to 10 minutes until the upper part is golden and the cheddar cheese melts.

13. Remove the dish from the oven.

14. Serve and garnish with green onions and chives.

Nutritional Information/serving

Calories 413 kcal, Protein 13.4g, Dietary Fiber 1.1g, Carbohydrates 5.8g, Fat 37.9g

Southern Keto Fried Green Tomatoes

Preparation Time: 15 minutes

Cook Time: 10 minutes

Serve: 6 servings

Ingredients

1/4 cup bacon fat

Fresh black pepper, ground

3/4 tsp salt

1/4 teaspoon cayenne pepper

1/2 teaspoon powdered garlic

1 teaspoon powdered onion

1 cup almond flour

2 tbsps water

1 large egg

2 medium green tomatoes (sliced into 1/4" thick)

Preparation

1. In a bowl, add in the sliced green tomatoes and season with a pinch of salt.

2. Set aside the green tomatoes for 5 minutes.

3. Add 2 tablespoons of water and egg into a small bowl and whisk together.

4. Add black pepper, salt, cayenne pepper, garlic powder, onion powder and almond flour into another bowl. Mix until combined.

5. On med-high heat, place a pan over heat and add in 1/4 cup of bacon fat.

6. In the egg bowl, dip each green tomato, remove and dredge into the almond flour bowl.

7. Remove the tomato slice from the almond flour mixture and get rid of the excess almond flour mixture by shaking lightly.

Note: Repeat the above coating process with the remaining green tomatoes slices.

8. Transfer the coated tomatoes slices into the heated bacon fat in the pan.

9. Cook each side of the tomatoes until brown, for 3 minutes to 5 minutes.

10. On a paper towel, transfer the cooked tomato slices to pat dry.

11. Season the fried green tomatoes with salt.

Note: The coated green tomato slices can be cooked in batches.

Nutritional Information/serving

Calories 57 kcal, Protein 2.9g, Dietary Fiber 1.3g, Carbohydrates 4.8g, Fat 3.5g

Southern Keto Tortillas

Preparation Time: 10 minutes

Cook Time: 5 minutes

Serve: 8 servings

Ingredients

3 tsps water

1 lightly beaten egg

2 tsps apple cider vinegar

1/4 tsp kosher salt

1 tsp baking powder

2 tsps xanthan gum

24g coconut flour

96g almond flour

Preparation

1. In a food processor, add in salt, baking powder, xanthan gum, coconut flour and almond flour.

2. Pulse the almond flour mixture until combined.

3. Add in the apple cider vinegar while the food processor is processing.

4. Process the almond flour mixture together until combined, add in water and the lightly beaten egg while the food processor is running.

5. Process until a ball of dough is formed.

6. In a cling film, transfer the dough and knead for 1 minute or 2 minutes through the plastic.

7. Set aside the kneaded dough for 10 minutes.

8. On med-heat, place a pan over heat.

9. Divide mixture into 8 (1 in.) balls. Using a tortilla press, flatten each dough ball between 2 parchment paper sheets until a 5" wide circle is formed.

10. Repeat the above process with the remaining dough balls.

11. Add the crust into the heated pan and cook for 3 seconds to 6 seconds.

12. Turn the tortillas with a knife and cook the other side, for 30 seconds to 40 seconds on each side, until it is slightly brown.

13. Transfer the tortillas onto a kitchen cloth and wrap to keep warm.

14. Store in an airtight container and place into the refrigerator for 72 hours.

Nutritional Information/serving

Calories 89 kcal, Protein 3g, Dietary Fiber 2g, Carbohydrates 4g, Fat 6g

Keto Coconut Flour Buns

Preparation Time: 15 minutes

Cook Time: 40 minutes

Serve: 4 servings

Ingredients

Pepper

Salt

1 cup water

1/2 tbsp apple cider vinegar

1 tsp baking powder

2 egg yolks

4 egg whites

2 tbsps psyllium husks (ground)

1/4 cup coconut flour

Preparation

1. Use parchment paper to line a baking pan and heat up the oven to 350°F.

2. Add the egg whites into a bowl, mix with a hand mixer until stiff peaks are formed and let stand.

3. In another bowl, add in salt, pepper, water, apple cider vinegar, baking powder, egg yolks, psyllium husks and coconut flour.

4. Lightly fold in the beaten egg whites into the flour mixture.

5. Divide the dough into 4 evenly thick sizes, roll each dough and transfer onto the lined baking pan.

6. Place the baking pan into the oven and bake until it is well cooked for 40 minutes.

7. Serve coconut flour buns warm.

Nutritional Information/serving

Calories 120 kcal, Protein 6g, Net Carbs 6.1g, Dietary Fiber 17.3g, Carbohydrates 23.4g, Fat 3.1g

Delicious Southern Keto Coleslaw

Preparation Time: 10 minutes

Cook Time: 0 minutes

Serve: 6 servings

Ingredients

Pepper

Salt

1 tablespoon swerve

1 teaspoon Dijon mustard

1 tablespoon lime juice

1 tablespoon apple cider vinegar

1/2 cup mayonnaise

1 (chopped) cabbage head,

1 (grated) carrot

Preparation

1. In a bowl, add in the chopped cabbage and grated carrot. Let stand.

2. Add pepper, swerve, Dijon mustard, lime juice, apple cider vinegar and mayonnaise in a medium bowl.

3. Mix together until swerve reaches a dissolved consistency.

4. Pour mayonnaise mixture over the salad and toss to coat.

5. Serve the Southern keto Coleslaw.

Nutritional Information/serving

Calories 178 kcal, Protein 3g, Dietary Fiber 7g, Carbohydrates 13g, Fat 14g

Southern Keto Fried Okra

Preparation Time: 10 minutes

Cook Time: 5 minutes

Serve: 5 servings

Ingredients

1/4 teaspoon pepper

1/4 teaspoon salt

1/3 cup almond flour

Beef tallow

1 pound Okra (fresh), removed stems and sliced into 1/4" slices.

Preparation

1. On a med-high heat, place a big heavy bottom skillet over heat and add in beef tallow about 1/4" of the skillet base.

2. Add the sliced okra, pepper, salt and almond flour into a medium bowl. Toss to evenly coat the sliced okra.

3. Transfer the coated okra into the heated beef tallow in the skillet and stir-fry until the okra is golden.

4. Transfer the fried okra to a paper towel and pat dry.

Nutritional Information/serving

Calories 130 kcal, Dietary Fiber 4g, Fat 10g, Protein 3g, Carbohydrates 7g

Pressure Cooked Mashed Cauliflower

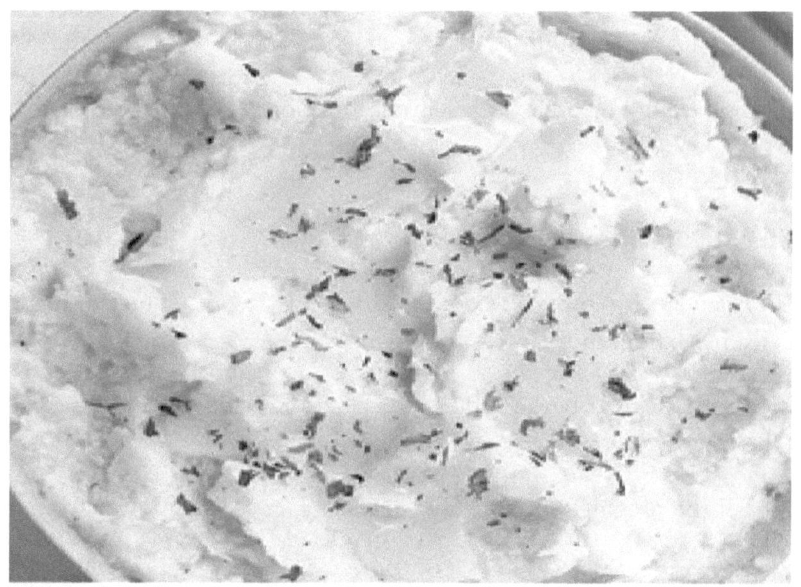

Preparation Time: 5 minutes

Cook Time: 8 minutes

Serve: 4 servings

Ingredients

2 (sliced) green onions

4 thick cut bacon slices (cooked until crisped & diced)

1/4 cup parmesan cheese, grated

3/4 cup cheddar cheese, shredded

Ground fresh pepper

Salt

1 tbsp sour cream

1/2 tbsp butter

1 garlic clove

1 1/2 cups chicken broth

1 large (remove core & coarsely cut into florets) cauliflower head

Preparation

1. Heat up the oven to 375°F.

2. In an electric pressure cooker, add in 1 1/2 cup of chicken broth. Place a steamer basket in the pressure pot.

3. In the steamer basket, add in the cauliflower florets and place a lid over the electric pressure cooker.

4. Set the pressure cooker valve to sealing, cook cauliflower for 3 minutes on high.

5. In a blender, add the cooked cauliflower florets and discard the liquid in the pressure pot.

6. In the blender, add in fresh pepper, salt, sour cream, butter and garlic clove. Pulse until the cauliflower mixture is creamy.

7. In a baking dish, add in the cauliflower mixture.

8. Sprinkle the diced bacon and cheeses over the cauliflower mixture.

9. Transfer the baking dish into the preheated oven and bake until the cheeses melts for 5 minutes.

10. Garnish with sliced green onions and serve.

Nutritional Information/serving

Calories 235 kcal, Protein 12g, Dietary Fiber 0g, Carbohydrates 1g, Fat 19g

Creamy Cheese Cornbread

Preparation Time: 10 minutes

Cook Time: 40 minutes

Serve: 12 servings

Ingredients

2/3 can (chopped) baby corn

1 cup cheddar cheese, shredded

25 drops stevia, liquid

1/4 cup sour cream

1/2 cup (melted) butter

3 large eggs

1 teaspoon Himalayan salt

3 teaspoons baking powder

1/4 cup coconut flour

2 cups almond flour

Preparation

1. Grease a casserole dish of 9" and heat up the oven to 350°F.

2. Add Himalayan salt, baking powder, coconut flour and almond flour into a medium bowl.

3. Whisk the almond flour mixture together and let stand.

4. Add stevia, sour cream, butter and eggs into a big bowl, whisk the mixture until a fine texture is reached.

5. Gently stir in the almond flour mixture into the butter mixture. Stir until combined.

6. Add in the baby corn and shredded cheddar cheese into the batter.

7. Transfer the batter into the greased casserole dish and place in the preheated oven.

8. Bake cornbread for 37 minutes to 40 minutes.

9. Set aside to for 15 minutes to cool.

10. Slice creamy cheese cornbread into 12 pieces and serve.

Nutritional Information/serving

Calories 254 kcal, Protein 8.4g, Dietary Fiber 3g, Carbohydrates 6g, Fat 22.7g

Delicious Keto Meatloaf

Preparation Time: 5 minutes

Cook Time: 60 minutes

Serve: 8 servings

Ingredients

1/2 cup ketchup (sugar free)

1/2 teaspoon powdered garlic

1 teaspoon dry mustard (ground)

1/2 teaspoon black pepper

1 teaspoon salt

1 tablespoon powdered onion

1 1/2 tablespoons Worcestershire sauce

3 large eggs

2 pounds beef (ground)

Preparation

1. Heat up the oven to 350°F.

2. Add garlic powder, mustard, black pepper, salt, onion powder, Worcestershire sauce, eggs and ground beef into a big bowl.

3. Stir together until the ground beef mixture combined.

4. In a 13 by 9" baking dish, form a loaf from the ground beef mixture.

5. Transfer the baking dish into the preheated oven and bake meatloaf for 45 minutes without covering the dish.

6. Take meatloaf out of the oven, add ketchup to the top and spread evenly.

7. Place the baking dish with the meatloaf back into the oven and bake until well cooked, for 15 minutes.

8. Set aside the meatloaf for few minutes to cool, slice and serve.

Nutritional Information/Serving

Calories 283 kcal, Protein 24g, Dietary Fiber 0g, Carbohydrates 2g, Fat 19g

END

Thank you for reading my book.

Adriana Hildebrandt